CULTURE
&
IDENTITY

Vol.2 – USA

Poetry exploring culture and identity, from
poets across the USA.

Compiled by Robin Barratt

THE POET

A leading international online poetry magazine, recognized for both its themed collections, and its interviews with poets worldwide; looking at their work and their words, and what motivates and inspires them to write.

www.ThePoetMagazine.org

~

CULTURE & IDENTITY
Vol. 2 - USA

Published by THE POET

ISBN: 9798414944836

E: Robin@ThePoetMagazine.org

Cover image and design: Canva
www.Canva.com

Compiled and published for THE POET by:
Robin Barratt Publishing
Affordable Publishing Services

www.RobinBarratt.co.uk

THE POET is sponsored by:

Poems Over
Coffee

John Johnson

www.PoemsOverCoffee.com

"John Johnson is a proud sponsor of THE POET."

If you would also like to sponsor THE POET, please go to:

www.thepoetmagazine.org/support-us

ALSO FROM THE POET

We produce some of the largest international anthologies on particular themes and topics ever published.

ADVERSITY: Volumes 1 & 2
FRIENDS & FRIENDSHIP: Volumes 1 & 2
FAITH: Volumes 1 & 2
CHILDHOOD: Volumes 1 & 2
CHRISTMAS – SPECIAL EDITION
A NEW WORLD - Rethinking our lives post-pandemic.
ON THE ROAD: Volumes 1 & 2
WAR & BATTLE
THE SEASONS
LOVE

CONTENTS

171.   Hanh Chau - CALIFORNIA
173.   Mark O. Decker - DELAWARE

"Cultural identity is a part of a person's identity, or their self-conception and self-perception, and is related to nationality, ethnicity, religion, social class, generation, locality or any kind of social group that has its own distinct culture."

Jan Ball
CHICAGO, ILLINOIS

Jan has had 357 poems published in various journals internationally and in the U.S. including: *ABZ, Mid-American Review, Parnassus* and *Puerto del Sol*. Finishing Line Press published her three chapbooks and first full length poetry collection, *I Wanted To Dance With My Father*. Orbis, England, nominated her for the Pushcart Prize in 2020. Besides her poetry, Jan wrote a dissertation at the University of Rochester: *Age and Natural Order in Second Language Acquisition* after being a nun for seven years then living in Australia for fourteen years with her Aussie husband and two children. Jan has taught ESL in Rochester, New York and Loyola and DePaul Universities in Chicago.
E: janiceball@usa.net

CATHOLIC REHAB

My sister pulls the blankets under her chin
as I feel I might explode from the radiator
heat in this Catholic rehab facility but she's
had a fever since they transferred her
from the hospital yesterday where she
survived the removal of an infected hip
replacement and abscess on the psoas muscle,
so far.

Many of her friends depicted in the hallways
to room 108, bed 2, are here recovering,
so empathize with her: Jesus sweating
in Gethsemane, as if he has the flu,
Mary in various depressive visages: swords
bursting from her heart as Mater Misericordia,
for one, and down the hall, St. Lawrence
with sores fit for a burn unit. I also recognize
pale St. Francis surrounded by docile wolves
and squirrels possibly rabid, as well as
St. Sebastian catching a draft in his underwear,
chest, arms and thighs speared with arrows,
St. Caecilia at her organ with her sliced neck
in need of a bandage and even Father Damian,
exposed to leprosy from his Molokai ministrations.

I know them all from another life when
I wore the habit, a "professional Catholic"
I like to say at dinner parties, sipping
Sauvignon Blanc then laughing. Now,
I don't believe in myths. However, just
this once, I need them to be true.

ABUELA'S FACE

Ximena is twelve when her *tia*
phones to say it's time to come
to the funeral parlour to put make-up
on her Grandma's inert face, a request
her *Abuela* made a few months ago,
Please, Ximena, you put the make-up
on my face when I die; the funeral
directors make a woman look
like a whore.

She goes to Grandma's house as quickly
as a pubescent girl can with dignity
and searches in Grandma's dressing
table drawer for base, blush, eyebrow
pencil, eye-liner, eye shadow, mascara
and the subdued pink lipstick she knows
Grandma keeps there.

At the funeral home, Grandma's skin
is leathery when Ximena holds her chin
securely as she smooths the base
across her Grandma's forehead
and tints her cheeks with blush.

The funeral director has closed
Grandma's eyes leaving pesos
on the eyelids to keep them secured,
so outlining them with eye-liner
and brushing mascara on Grandma's
eye-lashes is easier than she thought
it would be. Grandma's lipstick,
sticky to apply, looks natural
with just a little gloss.

Okay, Grandma, ready for viewing,
Ximena thinks, and smiles as she
kisses her Abuela's cold hands.

DANCING WITH ANDREW

I wanted to ask you if Andrew danced
last week at the talent show when
the South American students selected
some of us to join them on stage, trying
to mirror the way their supple, young
bodies pulsate with the Latin rhythms,
their hearts clearly beating beneath
their t-shirts resonating in their bones
like wind chimes, each of us swaying
our hips and rolling our shoulders
with our respective partners like Dancing
with the Stars, although, to tell the truth,
I didn't feel very sequinned, concentrating
on draping my arm over my Argentine
partner's shoulder then sliding it along
his collarbone like a silk scarf before he
rotated me like the ballerina on top of
my grandmother's music box. Frankly,
I didn't actually see you on the dance
floor with the pretty Chilean woman
who I noticed asked you to get up there
to wiggle with her, so focused was I on
my own enjoyment, almost hysterical as
an American teenager at a rock concert
with the unaccustomed rapid movement
of my feet to music, this socially-relaxed
atmosphere where foreign students invite
teachers to dance with them, and even
their director, you. Afterwards, walking
through the quiet corridors back to our
offices, you seemed pensive, slightly
cynical like Peter Sellers was supposed
to be in real life. I wanted to ask if you
danced with Andrew, but I couldn't.

Jeanine Stevens

SACRAMENTO, CALIFORNIA

Jeanine studied poetry at U.C. Davis, earned her M.A. at CSU Sacramento, has a doctorate in Education and is Professor Emerita at American River College. She is the author of *Limberlost and Inheritor* (Future Cycle Press). Her first poetry collection, *Sailing on Milkweed*, was published by Cherry Grove Collections. She is winner of the MacGuffin Poet Hunt, The Stockton Arts Commission Award, The Ekphrasis Prize and WOMR Cape Cod Community Radio National Poetry Award. *Brief Immensity*, won the Finishing Line Press Open Chapbook Award. Her most recent chapbook, *Gertrude Sitting: Portraits of Women*, won The Heartland Review 2020 Chapbook Award. She participated in Literary Lectures sponsored by Poets and Writers. Work has appeared in *North Dakota Review, Sentinel Literary Review, Dragonheart, Stoneboat, Rosebud, Chiron Review*, and *Evansville Review*. She is also a collage artist and has exhibited her work in various art galleries.
E: stevensaj@yahoo.com

RITE OF PASSAGE

According to a master gardener, my earth
needs mulch, compost. Yet every season
they disappear, clay eating away.
I'm left with fudge-like density.
The ancients say "Clay made of nutrients,
we are made of clay."

I admire a recent photograph,
men in levis, cowboy shirts and hats,
women in long dresses,
a four-day ceremony to celebrate
a young Apache woman's first menses.
She sits serious on layers of colorful blankets,
red, orange and blue. Her white dress
and necklaces disappear
under a thick layer of ochre-colored clay.
Hair already stiff, she will be reincarnated
as White Painted Woman,
a new mother of the tribe, as she emerges
out of this richness, stronger.

Almost fourteen, my turn came
on a bus trip from the Valley to Redondo Beach,
by way of Los Angeles—two transfers.
At the five and dime where my aunt works,
she quietly hands me supplies.
Back home, no mention, except,
"That's a shame." Anemic, low on iron,
I thought at least I would receive my favorite
chocolate layer cake, marshmallow
frosting, an entire jar
of maraschinos cherries on top.

LATE '50s

I could use a few of those nights,
on a whim drive over Topanga Canyon
to the beach grabbing silver grunion
or through scented orange groves
in the day-blue night sky.
I want one more dance
at the Hollywood Palladium,
and after, Travalini's on Ventura Blvd.
for steaming deep dish pizza.
Pinned on my wall, John Mathis
and Mario Lanza. Rossini's Tarantella
on the portable phonograph,
pink ballet shoes dangle
from the door knob. No thought
to the future, just the next disc—
          ~ Vido Musso on sax.

PINAFORE SUMMER

My sister and I were talking about how we weren't coddled as children. When young, I thought this normal. Most of my friends weren't coddled either. One summer Mother decided to have our pinafores hand made. A friend of Aunt Dorothy's was a good seamstress. Mother bought the fabric, bright pink cotton and green and white striped seersucker. We walked to have the fitting, early because by 11 a.m., the Midwest was already steamy. It took half an hour to get there and the fitting was fun. Mother had given me a grocery list for Kroeger's after we finished. This was a twenty-minute walk in another direction. At the market, I realized I lost the list. I did have money for the pay phone and called her. She was not happy, but said just get "Sugar, potatoes and flour." My sister, four years old, was red faced, glassy eyed. We drank water from the fountain at the gas station.

The pinafores were beautiful, the green my favorite. We packed them for our vacation to Bruce Lake. I made friends with a little girl who gave me plums. Delicious, but they dripped down the front of the pink bib. The next week, I was told to put it on for Sunday School even though there was a dark stain. Kids made fun of me; I got teary. The teacher took me to Haag's Drugs for ice cream; she felt sorry for me. She mentioned that she had dated our Uncle Charley when they were in church choir together. That was the last time I wore the pink pinafore.

D. R. James
SAUGATUCK, MICHIGAN

D. R.'s latest of ten collections are *Mobius Trip* and *Flip Requiem* (Dos Madres Press, 2021, 2020); his micro-chapbook *All Her Jazz* is free, fun, and printable-for-folding at the Origami Poems Project; and individual prose and poems have appeared in a wide variety of print and online anthologies and journals. James is a Pushcart and Best of the Net nominee, and several times the winner or near-winner of various individual poetry and book prizes. He is set to retire in May 2022 after 37 years of teaching writing, literature, and peace studies at a small college, and will continue working as a freelance writer and editor.

E: james@hope.edu
Instagram: @drjames1954
Amazon author page: @drjamesauthorpage

BEYOND COMPLIANCE, BEYOND RESISTANCE
When asked once who his greatest spiritual teacher had been the Dalai Lama responded, "China."

The cat's reactions to my fingers'
scratching, remind me I'm often
automatic: twitching skin of each
thank-you-very-much, arched back
of jockeying for a slender compliment,
submissive flop-and-grovel of every
please, please, please. But then

that prance of defiance across
invisible piano wire spanning
table to out-of-bounds countertop
to stove controls, my dainty paws,
claws approximately withdrawn,
picking out the touch-pad tune of
bake, broil, clean, clock, and cancel.

Lately I've been working on my
up-and-walk-away, my saunter
and dusty-sandal forefoot flick,
my vertical tail-like-a-flag of
nonchalance—which I plan to plant
somewhere pacifistic, somewhere
beyond this rage against my own Beijing.

First published in *Why War* (Finishing Line Press, 2014).

ASH WEDNESDAY

This life of separateness may be compared to a
dream, a phantasm, a bubble, a shadow, a drop
of dew, a flash of lightning. —The Buddha

The heat kicking in at precisely five a.m.
stirs the shirred glass chimes dangling over
the open vent, their fragile song reminding me
I am alone. Outside, where I know too-early

browns loom in the dark where constant white
should lighten this time of year—here, far
north of the end of Mardi Gras—one car
purrs by per hour. A semi ascending the hill,

up-shifting its dissonance across the cushion
of the dumb neighborhood, will turn left
at the next intersection, head east to open road,
and merge with the world. This separateness

is indeed a dream, though priests today will call
the many to mourn whatever separates them
from God and from each other, then swipe soaked
ash across their foreheads in remembrance that

we're all just dust. Which is true, but in this
blue mood I prefer the Buddha's drop of dew
and picture its sole self temporarily resting
upon a palm leaf before a breeze shivers it

earthward or the desert sun draws it skyward—
in either case to mingle it by absorption
or by evaporation into the eternal system
of one. Which is really only a better way

of getting it wrong. Poor sentient drop, alive
in the thought it has ever left its sisters and brothers,
who in their own dreams manufacture fantastic
bubbles but imagine wry shadow, or lightning.

First published in *Talking River 38* (Spring 2015).

ATOP MT. HARVARD, MAY 1976, WITH A LINE FROM MAJOR JACKSON

You must ascend a mountain to learn
your relation to matter. —Henry David Thoreau

The summit staged a glimpse. The West became
a canvas. When I'm dispersed, it draws back.
That chalked terrain: peaks pleated, engraved, cocked-
pinched infinity, fabric embroidered
with the white flares of lingering snowpack.
I thought, how else might I conjure heaven?
My mind's museumed, hammered facts, haloed
proofs, disturbed forever. Imagine them
clenching fists at infringement. They'd had god's
licensed niche, and the jig was all but up.

First published in *The Ravens Perch* (February 21, 2020)

Kashiana Singh
CHICAGO, ILLINOIS

When Kashiana is not writing, she lives to embody her *TEDx* talk theme of Work as Worship into her every day. She currently serves as Managing Editor for *Poets Reading the News*. Her chapbook *Crushed Anthills* by Yavanika Press is a journey through 10 cities. Her second full-length collection, *Woman by the Door* is coming out in 2022 with Apprentice House Press.
E: kashiana.singh@gmail.com
W: www.kashianasingh.com
FB: @authorkashianasingh
Instagram: @kashianasingh
Twitter: @Kashianasingh

MY NAME TOO

My name too ends with Singh
It too means brave, it too sings
My father wears a turban too
He too wears a beard
My aunts
they dance together
For every alien beat imagined
My uncles run open kitchens
For whenever America cries
They step up, step into—
        hurricanes or
        earthquakes, war zones
        for that is their way of life
        man to man and man to god
        the Sikh embodies actions
        that their ancestors taught.
They do.
They don't say
action lodges
in a Sikh's blood
so, they actioned
feeding endlessly
as the virus
raged tirelessly.
Sikh, fearless.
their wives and sisters, their
kaur daughters make curries
baking bread, sliced, or fried
the Sikhs gathered, fed God
through man, they never ask
they never have, they do, for
they do not care, for who you
were or what you were called.
they serve, seek humanity
just as their seers had taught
the same simple ways my mother
works her days, for she too taught
me some of the same, with folded
hands, "work is worship"
she said each morn
while she hummed
the prayer song

her spine straight
hands echoing spaces
she, my father, are as
Sikhs are—
One Sikh.
Oneness.
like every parent, they too say—
"Child, you must embody
what a Sikh truly means.
Oneness is what a Sikh holds.
Your muse is Him, none else.
Do not dread, dare to dream
stay in *Chardi Kalan*, always
no matter what, speak in a
kind voice, like the *Beas* of
your birth, flow into places."

They wore turbans too
working packages
on a chilly night
a coincidence maybe
it matters not, for
four Sikhs killed in
another random response.

I am a Sikh too
my name is Singh
I also bear Sikhs
My name is Singh

I wonder who is tracking my
wheels, I wonder why I need
to explain, their compassion
or the Singh's effervescence
I wonder when we will dare
to face the image
of man in man
not economize—
them
I wonder when encounters
of man to man will change
on the streets of America–
Black man, a Sikh man, or a
Brown man, Gay man, these
Different men, another man
Just being a student of man

Just hands holding up a sky
Be seekers, be Sikhs, seeking
Fedex facility-
their soup kitchen
feeds funerals

job posting-
$17 dollars an hour
all can apply

eight deceased victims.
Matthew R. Alexander, 32; Samaria Blackwell, 19; Amarjeet Johal, 66; Jasvinder Kaur, 50; Jaswinder Singh, 68; Amarjit Sekhon, 48; Karli Smith, 19; and John Weisert, 74

First published on *Poets Reading the News* – June 2021.

Michal Mahgerefteh
NORFOLK, VIRGINIA

Michal (Mitak) is an award-winning American/Israeli poet and artist. She is the author of five poetry chapbooks, two forthcoming in 2022, and is the managing editor of *Poetica Magazine* and *Mizmor Anthology.* She is an active member of The Poetry Society of Virginia and Voices Israel Poetry Group.
E: mitakart@aol.com
W: www.Mitak-art.com

BLESSINGS

At the entry gate in the old city of Rabat,
where the seed of my ancestors fell long ago.

Father's old eyes misting over my travel tale,
his childhood years in Morocco unreconciled ...

I long to tell him about the couscous I ate with bare
hands and the beauty of sidewalks in fig and palm;

the elderly man with a frayed cloth-cap who
followed me in the walkways of the bazaar;

about streets cramped with stray dogs and donkey
carts dusty towns built of cinder blocks, cement, sand;

how the housekeeper at the lodge sprinkled salt over
our bedroom floor before we slept each night.

A hint of interest, cafe hafuch poised to his lips,
"May your feet always walk on rose petals," he says.

STUDY

After Shacharit prayer on top of Masada fortress,
we drove in Father's battered Vespa scooter down
the Aravah Valley toward the old city of Jericho.

I sat in the sidecar, playing with the flowing
tassels of his tallit, watching the Moab Mountains
shading pools of pink and purple onto the Dead Sea.

He held my hand as we walked along the youngest
body of water, not a ripple on the glossy surface,
just points sparkling like crystals on salty formations.

Father recalled the importance of this land, "Turks
and Bedouin early history still stirs the prosaic shore,
always gives voice to the past. Study, and trace your roots."

*Shacharit - Morning Paryer

TISSUE

Walking down Kidron Valley at Mount Olives
was harsh on Father, over ninety degrees.
But he was determined to reach the slopes,

"Look at the beauty in the distance," he said,
exhibiting his vast knowledge. The rock-cut
tombs dated back to the 7th and 9th centuries BCE.

Black goats grouped under a solitary olive tree;
its hallowed trunk stood plagues, greeted the sun
and warriors over thousands of years. "Listen ..."

Father continued, offering me his skeletal
stories. But I didn't care about the arrival
of the Messiah or End of Days prophecy taking
place within the deepest tissue of the river below.

Madeline Artenberg
QUEENS, NEW YORK

Before falling for poetry, Madeline was a press-pass-carrying photojournalist and street theatre performer. Her poetry has appeared in many print and online publications such as *MacQueen's Quinterly, Rattle, Mudfish*, and *Literature Today International Journal*. *The Old In-and-Out*, a play based on her poetry and that of Karen Hildebrand, had a sold-out run in 2013. She won Lyric Recovery and Poetry Forum prizes; was Semi-Finalist in *Margie, The American Journal of Poetry* contest; Honourable Mention in the 2017 Highland Park Poetry Challenge; Finalist in *Mudfish* poetry contest 2020; and Best of the Net 2020-Nominee by Poets Wear Prada. Madeline is a regular feature on the New York City poetry circuit and has performed on *Barnard Radio, Columbia Radio, Teachers and Writers Collaborative* and on cable TV. For almost two decades, she had been co-producing The Alternative New Year's Day Spoken Word Extravaganza in New York City.
E: madderpoet@erols.com
E: madderpoet.MA@gmail.com
FB: @Madeline.Artenberg

AT ELLIS ISLAND

they throw away
my father's last name. He covers
his Sephardic roots, blends in
with the Eastern European Jews.

He settles family in a Brooklyn project.
When father smells one whiff
of cumin-laced lamb, he closes
our windows, piles on his plate
brisket and boiled potato.

When he comes upon neighbours, he brushes
past their *Komo estash*, mutters
under his breath, "I'm fine, I'm fine."

When his daughter asks where he was born,
he points far across ocean.
She collects photos of faces like his:
long and narrow, high-cheek bones,
sharp chin, dark eyes.

In school, she slips easily into *Me llamo.*
Señoritas in red beckon
from grammar books. When she decides
to teach Spanish, father yells,
"You're throwing away your education."

Now, he's lost the way
to temple, can't find the next
prayer page.

Every day, she shows him photos
of faces like his. He's forgotten
who she is, forgotten his name.
Every day, he prays,
"Dío, por favor,
take me
to mi padre."

BATTER

The last time I saw Grandma's
dark eyes, they were empty
bowls.

When I was a girl, I imagined
her flying across ocean
from a land where everyone was rooted
like trunks cut in half. Better
to have thought of her
springing from bowls of batter
than from between thighs squatting
above a dirt road.

I imagined her arriving here
with perfect English. But,
when I asked, "Where'd you
come from? How'd you
get here?" she said, "OK."
When I complained about math—
she went "ptoo, ptoo, ptoo,"
told her about the monster
in the closet—she smiled.

It was enough to hug Grandma's
box of a body, tower
over her when I was seven, wrap
my arms almost twice around her
as I pressed my cheek to hers.

Together, we worked
the challeh dough—
my long, pale arms—
her dark, small ones—intertwined
like braids. Sometimes, I snatched
a still-baking bread
from the oven, devouring
the centre.

Previously published: *Literature Today*, 2018.

OLD PICTURES

My grandmother would have carried
grandfather if her back
were better.
She did everything else
for him.

After her death,
the police kept hauling him
lost and bewildered back to our house.
He crawled out again and again
to look for her.

My mother-in-law tended
to her starched husband.
She died still praying
he would go first.

But for nosey neighbours,
he would've starved facing
food-filled cupboards.

I sit in front of two laden
plates on the kitchen table.
My husband is very late—
his key turns in the door.
He's pleased I haven't eaten.

Donna Pucciani
CHICAGO, ILLINOIS

Donna has published poetry worldwide in *Acumen, Agenda, Gradiva, Meniscus, Shi Chao Poetry, Poetry Salzburg, Journal of Italian Translation*, and other journals. Her grandparents and emigrated to New York from southern Italy in the early 1900s. Their story, and her cultural heritage, are documented in her poetry chapbook, *Ghost Garden*. Pucciani's seventh and most recent book of poetry is titled *Edges* (Purple Flag Press).
E: dpucciani@yahoo.com

EMBELLISHMENTS

Inside Giuseppina,
lace waits to emerge,
elegant ribbons spooling
from her dark interior. Her wrinkled
body becomes fabric, her eyes
eyelets behind milky cataracts.

Yards of white
stacked shoulder to shoulder
come unbolted
in the dimly-lit territory
of ancient Italian women
shopping for something beautiful
among caged chickens, brine-barreled olives.

At home, Giuseppina creates
a hope chest for three granddaughters.
Among scratchy white towels
and unblemished muslin folded
tight and thick among the mothballs,
lie pillowcases painfully plain.

Giuseppina edges them with embroidered
scallops and shells. She pedals
the black iron Singer, trestles stitching
cotton on cotton, thinking of
the old country, the village, the sea.

Her treasures lie hidden, emerge discolored
years later on beds where cheap
brightly-colored sheets
lie back and open themselves
to white butterflies.

THE BEE IN THE FLOWER

Like the bee supping the tulip that pushes red lips
through soil to kiss the first early week of spring,
I taste delight, try to hold it fast amid the hum

of fragile wings. Only a miracle
could make the moment stay, but who would want
the last slow days of dying to stretch us

on the rack forever? An uncle once advised,
Be careful what you wish for.
The passage of time tumbles us

breathless in the wake of joy, or struggling
on death's dark edge. In the time it takes for me
to fasten a strand of windblown hair, or smell rain

on a hilltop in Italy, gasping in gladness
at the village of my nonno, a bee gathers honey
from the bell of a flower and disappears.

In the deep snow of a prairie night, such sweetness
cannot be forgotten, cannot be resurrected
except in sleep, where the song of the mountain

pours like nectar onto my pillow, into
the brain's unconscious cup of heaven,
into my honeycombed dreams.

TREASURES

At home in Bergamo,
with Carmen's quiche of prosciutto and provolone
in the oven, we gather in the next room
to touch the varnished maple chest
from our grandfathers' peasant village.

Pasquale takes out the ornate lock and key,
fashioned a hundred years ago,
that guards a jewelled clip for bisnonna's hair,
a handful of sepia photos, a watch with a broken face
on a gold chain, the smell of old wood,
and songs of the sea.

Carole Stone
NEW JERSEY

Distinguished Professor of English and creative writing, emerita, Montclair State University, Carole's poetry collections include *Hurt: The Shadow, All We Have Is Our Voice* (Dos Madres Press), *American Rhapsody* (Cavankerry Press), and *Traveling With The Dead* (Backwaters Press). Recent journal publications include *Crosswinds, Sequestrum* and *Pen and Brush*. She has received three Fellowships from The New Jersey State Council on the Arts, and her work has been nominated for the Pushcart Prize.
E: stonec@mail.montclair.edu

O, NEW JERSEY

Sundays, on Route 1 driving to Carteret
to see our Hungarian relatives, Jews on one side
of town, Catholics on the other,
my brother, cousin and I in the Packard's back seat
fought over who had to sit in the middle on the way home.

Smoke from Aunt Elsie's Pall Malls mingled
with Esso's oil tank fumes.
We drove on Route 36 past Keansburg
to the rented house in Bradley Beach.

All summer, we rode bikes, walked the boardwalk
through Ocean Grove we called Ocean Grave,
gates shut at midnight, no cars allowed on Sundays.
We laughed at old blue-haired women who rocked

on front porches. In Asbury Park we played
pinball, ate frozen custard.
We didn't understand what happiness meant
but smelled it in the salt air, the surf high,

the sun warm, before we had to return
to our aunt and uncle's house.
O, New Jersey, where Sinatra's voice is sacred
as Mass, I crossed your border
my suitcase packed with grief,
your chemical skyline a tear in my eye.

HOME OF THE BRAVE

Nobody knows the trouble I seen.
— African American Spiritual

Every morning in homeroom,
hand over my heart,
I pledged allegiance to the flag.

There were no African-Americans,
no Asians in my classes.
Japanese-Americans were interned

in camps far from New Jersey
in western states I'd never visited.
I went off to college,

picketed and marched in the America
of trouble. The cops show up
while you wait for a business meeting.

You're Black
so you must be up to something.
Something, something.

That's the trouble:
there's always something.
America.

HOPE

Friends keep disappearing;
some move south, others' names adorn stones.
Soon I'll be the only one left

who remembers Pathé newsreels,
German tanks rolling into Warsaw,
refugees on country roads

strafed by the Luftwaffe.
This century's like the last:
war, displacement, hatred.

Migrants flee on rubber boats,
women in headscarves, men in prayer caps.
Slaughter everywhere.

Summer beginning, the world starts up
again, hope a pianist
who can't stop playing.

Joseph Estevez
NEW YORK

Joseph started writing fiction at around the age of five. After graduating from high school, he started reading literary journals and magazines, at first to get a taste of contemporary fiction, but as they contained poetry, he came to appreciate it as well. He quickly started writing his own poetry. He graduated from City College in 2018. In 2021, he published his first book, *Poems*. It featured poetry with many themes, ranging from nature, to spirituality. He finished a second poetry collection, *Poems, Book Two*, this time dealing more with themes related to Judaism. This second collection deals with topics such as trust in God, having a relationship with Him, and His dominion over the world.
E: josephestevez9@gmail.com
Amazon Author Page: @Joseph-Estevez/e/B08YKFLM5Y

ISRAEL

My, oh my
What glistening land
Filled with holiness
What do you look like?
I have never seen your face
But only in my dreams
So far away
Farther than I've ever been
When will He bring me to you?
Only in my dreams
But at least I have this
A home
A true home
All else is temporary
I keep this in mind
Though I take joy in the journeys,
When will I return?
I have read of you
I have heard of you
But when will I return?
What must I do?
I can only wait

First published in *Poems* (2021).

FOREIGN

In this foreign land
Set aside for our allotment
This Holy Tongue
I have rarely spoken
These first fruits
Which I cannot give
All of these belong to me
Yet divorced from them I remain

Of these mighty heroes
Long gone before
These prophets and kings
Who walk the earth no more
The Temple which once stood
Has been taken away
We have been separated
By distance and time

What is mine?
The language I speak now,
The land I inhabit,
Or that of my distant fathers?
I have my inheritance
I must continue my cultivation
Of a garden commenced before
For its completion

First published in *Poems* (2021).

THE GREATEST ADVENTURE

The greatest adventure
Going through mountains
In ancient times
Yes, this is time travel
Yes, this is teleportation
To another place
Where we met with kings
And listened to the words of the prophets
Whose teachings are always binding
And we roamed through deserts
And fled to the hills of Judea
And crossed over the Jordan
When we came to see and hear
What happened in those years

First published in *Poems* (2021).

Krikor Der Hohannesian
MEDFORD, MASSACHUSETTS

Krikor is of Armenian descent, his forebears having fled the Turkish genocide. His poems have appeared in over 175 literary journals including T*he Evansville Review, The South Carolina Review, Atlanta Review, Louisiana Literature, Connecticut Review, Comstock Review* and *Natural Bridge*. He is a three-time Pushcart Prize nominee, and the author of two chapbooks *Ghosts and Whispers* (Finishing Line Press, 2010) and *Refuge in the Shadows* (Cervena Barva Press, 2013), as well as a full-length book, *First Generation* (Dos Madres Press, 2020). *Ghosts and Whispers* was a finalist for the Mass Book awards poetry category in 2011.
E: krikorndh@verizon.net

PASSAGE TO ARARAT
For Michael J. Arlen

Walking on stones
with soles bared, that's
what it must have been like.
Your pilgrimage, antithesis
of your father's on the winding
pocked road of the diaspora – Plovdiv,
Paris, London ... he chose
anglophilia, changed his name,
became an English dandy,
writer of British romances spoken
with Oxfordian perfection. Worse yet,
the mocking of his forebears as "quirky"
and besides, "the language was impossible".
His identity, and yours, doused
with the acid of his shame, vaporized.

Brave soul, you chose the journey –
the one he would never imagine.
The road back - Yerevan!, where
the eternal flame burns, where
you tossed a yellow rose
into the burning oil, your tears
a cascade down your cheeks
like snowmelt from the slopes
of Ararat - the tears your father
could never shed.

CABARET

everyone ogles the bellydancer,
who is certainly worth watching,
if that's what you came for.

frenetic hands whirl
cutting imaginary parabolas,
the blue smoke-haze caressed
into seductive curlicues.

the staccato clack of finger cymbals
punctuates the frenzy of hips, tempting
paunchy middle-aged men to stuff neatly
creased dollar bills under skimpy straps,
others bolder yet ...

but I am drawn to another pair of hands
flailing a dumbek, pounding out
a primal rhythm that reaches
across the ocean of red-clothed tables
calling, calling ...

TAVLOU

O grand ancient game, upholder of
family honour, Judas to reputations. Your
board a replica of Byzantine splendour, in-laid
mother-of-pearl, Javan teak points, die of
African ivory – we learned your caprices early,

toughened our psychic skins against barrages
of insults, learned to play fast and snap
the checkers, memorized Turkish terms –
shesh besh, penge u du, du barrah –
called with each throw. Curse the dice
for ill fortune, but count out your move
and you were unworthy. Uncle fixed me

with baleful stare the first time I took
his measure. Father swore he would never
play me again. Hairig, grandfather so gentle,
once bit the dice in frustration. Mother
at 92 took me – a wry smile in victory,
gone a week later.

Kate Falvey

NEW YORK

Kate's work has been fairly widely published in an eclectic array of journals and anthologies; in a full-length collection, *The Language of Little Girls* (David Robert Books); and in two chapbooks, *What the Sea Washes Up* (Dancing Girl Press) and *Morning Constitutional in Sunhat and Bolero* (Green Fuse Poetic Arts). She co-founded (with Monique Ferrell) and edited the *2 Bridges Review*, published through City Tech (City University of New York) where she teaches, and is an associate editor for the *Bellevue Literary Review*.

E: katefalvey@gmail.com

CATHOLIC CHARITIES

1. Class Act: Initiation

My new communicant wriggles her floral wreath
into askew, express position,
renegade curls already losing steam,
wisping their guileless sheen through the
gauzy distraction of veil and bud, the whites
rucked and layered with the prim,
beguiling petulance of girly yesteryears. Christ
likes little girls. I remember that. I
always thought that He would welcome me,
despite his Lordly penchant for
a gracious tit for tat. Could
I please Him with my tight little bonnet
of over-permed hair? My pin-tucked bodice?
The sheer inflation of my shuddering sleeves?
My devotional distress
makes a mess of my
deportment, slick-soled shoes
keep me bound to earth and floor -
it is miles to the altar, an aisle of
cold stone and trembling faces,
a slippery temptation
for missteps along the way.
Kneeling into organdy and adrenalin,
as the salver glints a thin reproval
at my neck, I
take in the papery
magnitude of the host,
ashamed of my instant
of undisguised distaste.
Maureen and I, adjacent, widen eyes,
exchange looks of mutual misgiving,
in communion, in cahoots. How in the world
can our Lord Jesus taste like this
dab of melting indefiniteness –
no real bite or substance, no distinction,
no surprise,
no sacrificial flavor of amazement or redress
Nothing but tongue-tamped
nothingness,
a paste of grace and ever-welling need.

Now, a life-time of hosts hence,
I wonder what we thought would be our prize:
jujubes in a darkened movie house,
the extra thrill of the teeny indent, small as a fairy's
tongue-print, stickily resistant
in the gleamy candy's center,
the worn velvet nap of the abundant springy seats,
the crinkly hush, the first blast of promise
from the mesmerizing screen. What comparisons
had we for awe and intimacy, for the quake and calm
of mounting expectations fully met?
The little grief in that godly let-down
probably did us good.
Or so the grownup in me says,
regularly toughened and
slick with sloughing losses,
even when I remember with terrible urgency,
my father's fingers loose and assured on the steering wheel,
my mother in darkened profile, a haze of black hair
flickering beautifully in and out of the gray night drive,
the highway lamps dazzling the snow in cones of joyous light.
The backseat was heaven.
We were pulling Christmas back with us,
over the radiant bridge,
Grandma's powdery cream puffs, Papa's special water dosed
with a thimble-full of wine,
the yards of minty blue tree lights trailing behind,
the noise, the gifts, the chattering crinolined and serge-suited
cousins,
the long line of narrow pushed-together tables,
draped with white cloths,
filling the whole of the mirrored living room,
laden with talk and bread crumbs, specks of sauce, strings
from the roast, a stray leaf from the triumphant platter of artichokes,
tangerine skins, walnut shells, the tiny cups of bitter coffee,
and looking up at Grandma, framed by fire escape and sill, waving as
we
bumped bags of toys and leftovers over the old Bronx cobblestones
to the old gold, snow-bleared Impala.
Settled in the perfect back seat, thickened with scarf and earflap,
I could almost see
Grandma's glazy ceramic wise men,
elate and strained with wonder,
following us wearily home.
The ponderous camel, the donkey

nested in the straw,
the pink and gold baby grown chubbily into his halo,
his perfect blue mama gazing transcendently on –
then, rising up from the snow, the road, the streaming movement
of illumined homes and trees, the delicious muzzy memories of
grownup din and ribbons, kisses, doll and scooter,
Papa making teeth and eyeglasses from the tangerine skins,
cradles from the walnut shells, blessings from the holy water
flung from last Easter's woven palm, extra drops of
misty absolution shaken in the face of one
chosen scapegrace child – rising clear as Mary's brow,
sweet as the last flake of peppermint already distant on the tongue –
my mother's voice carols a warm soprano Silent Night
and the world is truly still.

My little girl – child of my almost-too-late age –
sweeps into precious sight, a blur of veil and winsome grins,
and I click furiously.
Let this be
for her
for keeps.

Previously published in *Italian Americana*, 2012.

FOR MY DAUGHTER'S SIXTH GRADE HERITAGE PROJECT

So you're squeezing out the Irish,
the Italian shouldering in
and carrying the day, as mostly,
it did mine,
though I am half and half and not
three quarters as you are.

It wasn't
that the Irish side was less
a source of child's pride --
the name, the ruddy skin,
the crooked grins, the blarney --
but they were insubstantial,
had no staying power – those
Eileens and Kathleens. They were
sepia toned, hazy,
even when they, and I, were young;
I'd peer into their gatherings
as if from a harbor wharf
while they cast off, coasted, faded,
no berth on board for me.
Even my handsome Dad,
whose family this was,
seemed bleary-eyed and dated,
hopelessly at sea.

The Italians were weighted
with Grandma and Papa,
and long tables set end to end for miles
across the familiar cousin-rich country
of the North Bronx apartment living room,
a piece of bread dipped in the simmering sauce,
a glint of red wine in the small stemmed glass,
the women heading table-ward with white cloths,
white plates, to the tune of
Grandma's signal call:
"Pat –Pasquale--,
should I throw the macs?
How much should I throw?"
All poised after that,
settling into our accustomed seats,
awaiting Grandma's entrance

with the giant bowl of tortiglioni
which she'd ladle into bowls passed
uncle to cousin to aunt, then
hand to hand, the grated Parmigiano,
the hunks of bread,
the dishes of braciole, meatballs, salsiccia,
the gravy boats of extra sauce, melding
into the next course – some sort of roast
with vegetables – asparagus or beans –
tomatoes if in season, sliced,
in olive oil and basil,
a curly mess of tousled salad greens -
The artichokes, which Papa stuffed himself,
just like he did the mushrooms,
were carried in on platters like dessert,
snipped leaves crisped with garlic, salt, and oil,
trimmed stems steamed inside the chokes,
a surprise green olive inside a random few,
which I remember somehow always finding.
And through the ebbing afternoon,
the grownups' voices dimming
as the streetlamps wavered on,
the white cloths strewn with walnut shells,
tangerine skins, spills of sauce and wine,
the taste for plenty fused
with being sated,
not with food alone
but food suffused with time.

Previously published in *Feile-Festa*, 2013.

Mary Marie Dixon

HASTINGS, NEBRASKA

Mary, a visual artist and poet, has published creative and academic works in various periodicals and anthologies, and a collection of poetry, *Eucharist, Enter the Sacred Way*, (Franciscan University Press, 2008). Her focus is on women's spirituality and the mystics, combined with the Great Plains and the spiritual power of nature. She has exhibited her visual work and accompanying poetry in galleries, and explores the visual and poetic intersection in her creative life. She loves stars, sunrises, and sunsets on the open plains!

E: maryangelmead@yahoo.com
FB: @Mary-Marie-Dixon/104361173006800

PIECED

Here in a place far from Eden,
Home of stunted fertility,
This is a promised land stung with bees.

By the sweat of our brows.
Should we work the oath as my mother did
Razing thorns and gutting chickens?
Sacrificing our own comfort?
Her labour, by no means, unproductive
Her hands gnarled the bread in tight coils
Her skin yeasting as the promise bound itself to pain.

Here now, we glean what we can
Ever mindful that there is something lost.
Yet something is gained
Grandmother and great grandmother
And countless others
Still bearing witness though dead and gone
So we swathe ourselves in the heat
Drawn from their pieced together quilts

WHETSTONE

When he pioneered
this stretch of homestead
in the Little Blue Valley,

Grandfather bought
the whetstone with the axe
because he understood
the shape of wear.

With the axe
he notched beams,
and formed his cabin.

Father kept the treddle
oiled because he
recognized the shape of disuse.

The revolving whetstone
in its edging renewal
solved the dulling effort
and the dampening rest.

To inherit the wild
proliferation of rust was easy,
but to battle it
was exacting.

Domesticated,
the soul decays
in red dust
like the tines of a harrow.

wildflowers
diminish in
the cultivation
of dust.

Grandfather surrendered
the habits of reason
to the incomprehensibility
of virtue.
Like the axe,

shining from the whetstone,
my father mirrored
felled cottonwood.

Father's hands callus;
Grandfather's calluses
wear smooth.

Each stroke
smoothes
the axe handle.

The revolving stone
sharpens the blade,
the treadling stroke
hones the soul.

Nancy Shiffrin

SANTA MONICA, CALIFORNIA

Nancy is the author of *The Vast Unknowing*, poems (Infinity Publishing, 2012, BN.com.) She earned her BA at California State College, Northridge, her MA studying with Anais Nin. She earned her PhD at The Union Institute studying Jewish-American women authors. Her writing has appeared in the *Los Angeles Times, New York Quarterly, Earth's Daughters, Lummox Journal, The Canadian Jewish Outlook, A Cafe in Space, Religion and Literature, Shofar*, and numerous other publications. She has received awards and honourable mentions from The Academy of American Poets, The Poetry Society of America, The Alice Jackson Foundation, The Dora Teitelboim Foundation and Lummox Journal. Two new poetry collections, *Flight* and *Game with variations* are forthcoming
E: nshiffrin@earthlink.net
W: www.NancyShiffrin.net

LEARNING THE LANGUAGE

"what is God?"
Carlos crawled across three borders
to reinvent the Deity
he grapples with English
the babble which crafts new idols every season
will not capitalize the "J" in Judaism
rejects the Lord of Judgment
Spanish failed to cleanse him of questions
"God doesn't cause everything" Carlos insists
"we don't need His sympathy
'the wind cannot be grasped yet the wind exists'"

"Poems!
you did not forsake me in my burning hour
like a nurse you watched over and fed me
bread and water of my thirsty young life
when I lay ill you soothed my nightmares
when I first sat up in my sickbed you stood around me
laughed in small shaky sentences"
Malka Lee composed first in German
harsh trumpet of Almighty's demise
she rescued her pearls from burning and drowning
carried them over the sun-kissed blushing sea
she wrote about the Jew selling apples
clobbered by a Pole in broad daylight
the shtetl trembled while the killer went free
Malka did not beg compassion
but danced with the dead man's spirit
transposed herself into *yiddish mamaloshen*
of womens' prayer privacy rebellion

"I have lost God yet I speak the language of God!"
Amichai opens his performance
"'*Elohim* has pity on kindergarten children
for the grown man on his knees in the desert none'"
he chants *loshen hachodesh* bows slightly
becomes again a schoolboy
tallit draped over short trousers sticky between his legs
he won't write about the *Holocaust*
or reveal secrets of the *Mossad*
he can't forgive the faith which bled from his gut
on the way to the first-aid station

60

the enemy's vacant eyes
"we were created then abandoned" he sobs
yet is happy in his pants with the wife
whose cries progress from turtle-dove to eagle
whose shoes point away from the bed

I learn The Holy Letters
which parted the waters divided Heaven from Earth
the letters without which I cannot
know myself or place myself in time
I struggle to recognize shapes imitate sounds
I yearn for number and story
I must be careful
to look through my bifocals at just the right angle
I am too easily distracted by children skating
speech spiced with Armenian Russian Farsi
unwitting recipients of the mercy I beg for

Previously published in *The Vast Unknowing*, and in the journal *Religion and Literature*.

Suellen Wedmore
ROCKPORT, MASSACHUSETTS

Suellen, Poet Laureate emerita for the small seaside town of Rockport, Massachusetts, has been widely published. She has been awarded first place in the Writer's Digest's Rhyming Poem and Non-Rhyming Poem Contests. Her chapbook *Deployed* won the Grayson Press annual contest, her chapbook *On Marriage and Other Parallel Universes* was published by Finishing Line Press, and her chapbook *Mind the Light* won a first place in Quill's Edge Press' "Women on the Edge" contest. In 2014 she won first place in the Studios of Key West Contest, and three of her poems have been nominated for a Pushcart Prize. She graduated from the MFA Program in Poetry at New England College in 2004.
E: suellenwedmore@comcast.net

IN A THIMBLE OF MY SPIT
—after receiving the results of genetic testing

The surprise was this: if *23 and Me* were to offer a report card,
I would receive an A in Neanderthal: 297 markers—
you might assume I'd be upset, believing as I did that free will

rather than genetics had carried me nicely into my adult years,
but you would be wrong, for that evening, in my fire-lit kitchen,
as I sipped a glass of Don Ramon, I saw him, Grandpapa

to the 250th power, born a mere 64,000 years ago, in Spain
(or what it was then). He was low-browed but handsome,
fur stitched tight across a boxy chest, wearing deerskin leggings

and ragged leather shoes stuffed with straw to insulate him
from the frost-hard ground. Was my ancestral Granny250th, then,
dragged screaming from a nearby tribe of mysterious Homo sapiens?

Did he scare her into silence with bear-like growls, or did he whisper
her into a new life? Or was it, perhaps, Great-Grandmama
who swam across a roiling river to reach him, attracted

by his firm stance, his agile hands? I imagine him an aspiring artist,
imprinting a cave wall with an ochre handprint, lifting a boar-bristle
brush
to abstract a bison, a mammoth, images from plain, field and sky.

If he can be called up like this from a drop of DNA, should I not sense
his presence now and then, as I stumble into a dark woods,
trip into an unlighted room, or hear a rustle in the rangy grass?

A coyote's howl triggers adrenaline, quivering legs, a racing heart.
 Something in me remembers that I have been running
from predators for thousands of years: from lions, from tigers,

from angry neighbours, a raging sedan. From a neighbour,
suburban sycophant, or corporate captive—
Grandpapa! For you, for me: sanctuary is a glowing fire.

THE ICEMAN COMETH
—after visiting the Iceman Exhibit at the Museum of Archaeology,
Bolzano, Italy.

Ötzi: Freeze-dried & copper-skinned,
        you played hard-to-get in a prehistoric
hide and seek, waiting five thousand years

        to be found, head thrust out of a glacier's
warming, an arrowhead buried in your shoulder,
        eye sockets empty, left arm awry.

Pulled from ice, we greet you, frost-
        cocooned behind museum glass,
fingers curved as if for a long nap.

        Born before the pyramids rose at Giza,
before Stonehenge circled Salisbury Plain,
        I try to imagine you in your prime–

making love, crying, singing,
        all those things that make us human;
(mankind ingenious, even then

        judging from your fine-stitched coat,
your leggings of supple goatskin).
        You carried necessaries unavailable

to us now, even schooled
        as we are, industrialized, computerized:
you fashioned arrows from viburnum limbs,

        built a fire each night from embers
nestled in leaves in a birch bark urn,
        & sewn by an agile hand

with lime tree bast. They gave you a name
        to make you seem more human,
though your shoes did this for me—hay

        tucked around your feet with netting,
a leather strip across the sole for grip,
        grit for a hostile world.

A CHILD WAITING

to be born into sunlight & air,
        an egg speared by a fish-tailed gamete
encoding Ecuadorian eyelashes,

        de Vinci cheekbones, my own
boney-sharp knees. This will be
        all our futures crying into a hospital's

fluorescent gleam, with dark eyes,
        from a history not my own,
the drumbeat of the Andes, bamboo pipes,

        a hacienda's black-haired child
flirting beneath a eucalyptus.
        Soon an infant will curl

in my arms, smelling of dried milk
        & tomorrow. A world I will
someday not be part of. Singing.

Louis Girón
ASHEVILLE, NORTH CAROLINA

Louis is a recovering neurologist/clinical pharmacologist. He grew up in San Antonio, was a battalion surgeon in Vietnam, somehow endured several winters in the uninhabitable Midwest before coming to Asheville in western North Carolina, where neighbourhood bears, instead of rattlesnakes, greet him at the mailbox. After a completed poem dropped without warning into a budget for a research proposal, null hypotheses morphed into villanelles, dose-response curves into sonnets, and action potentials into palindromes. What began as a sign of mental infirmity now continues as necessity. His poems have appeared in *Aji, BathHouse Journal, Chest, Perihelion, Redactions, Revue (Kansas City), Still Point Arts Quarterly, Smoky Blue Literary and Arts Magazine, Snapdragon, Songs of Eretz, Sunflower Petals, The Amsterdam Quarterly, The Great Smokies Review, The New Guard Literary Review, The New Millennium, The Potomac, The Same, VietNow, Warscape*, and *Winning Writers*.
E: elgiron@aol.com

SAN ANTONIO

Every Texan has two homes and, in the Spring, one or both must be San Antonio;
home as well to cottonwoods, mesquite, riverbanks, uniforms, and *canciónes*;
refuge also to Los *Tres Colores*, scorpions, and the scents of pepper, *barbacoa y canela*.
Before *conquistadores* and missions, before Nueva España, there was the river and the heat.
The river, *un borracho*, weaves then staggers to the flourishes of the guitarras.
Follow the peoples of the *guitarras*, from past to present, listen to *palmas* and Spanish.

Sometimes rapid/riveting, or languid/sing-song, ever dramatic in cadence, Spanish
washes the streets, *el mercado, cantinas*; as water to rain, as necessary to San Antonio
and as inescapable as honey-suckle, magnolias, marijuana promises, and *guitarras.*
At night *La Llorana* glides through the streets, returns in shadows, dreams, and *canciónes*;
at noon, flies take siestas, eyeballs sizzle in sockets, while none — or all, talk of the heat.
After "pickles", unsuspecting *turistas* gulp Dos Equis, then *sopapillas* with *miel y canela*.

On river floats, señoritas, roses in hair, flash white teeth and skin the color of canela.
Fiesta, like a *quinceñera*, celebrates life. During Fiesta, all else stops. Parades and Spanish
rhythms celebrate Spring returning to the land; all beseech *la fortuna* to temper the heat.
Along the streets of La Villita, a river of trilled rr's flows in the heart of San Antonio.
Selena is gone, Tú Sóló Tú remains. Texan wannabes from New York nod to *canciónes*:
todos sombreros, no vaqueros; but they eat rattlesnake steak; dance in time to *guitarras*.

Gringos join *colonos*, sing *tejano*, relish jalapeños and *salsa verde*; they believe *guitarras*
and *corridos* make the good life as do blue bonnets and the polka.

Chocolate with *canela,*
enchiladas and margaritas vanish quickly; bands wheeze out
pasodobles y canciónes;
bougainvilleas cascade over fences; contrails lace the clouds. English and Spanish
mingle as sons and daughters of the Union, Confederacy, and Mexico join in San Antonio,
the descendants of the besiegers and of the defenders of the Alamo together in the heat.

WALKING HOME WITH CELLO AND ENDPIN

Home was short blocks away.

Running or sneaking by,
taking a different route, any
choice could bring a beating
or shake down.

Glasses had painted
the skinny kid a target.
He had learned how to run
and when he had to fight.

The first day of cello,
he walked from school
on knife fighter's feet;
cello, a heavy shield,

canvass strap to case
biting the left shoulder;
right hand, palm below,
tightly holding

the detached endpin,
sharp, gleaming,
metal point leading,

the duelling position,
a distorted inverted image,
he was to learn,

of the hand above the bow.

Ann Privateer
CALIFORNIA

Ann is a poet, artist, and photographer. Her work has appeared in a number of publications including *Third Wednesday, Entering* and *MindFull*.
E: annprivateer@gmail.com

THE AWAKENING

New consciousness
Unearthed, new blood
From lost youth, they
Took to the road
To tell their story.

No high school jackets
Class rings, class anything's
They became foragers
Of selfhood, those
That never sell out.

Ed Ahern
CONNECTICUT

Ed resumed writing after forty odd years in foreign intelligence and international sales. He's had over three hundred stories and poems published so far, and six books. Ed works the other side of writing at *Bewildering Stories*, where he sits on the review board and manages a posse of six review editors.

E: salmonier@aol.com
FB: @EdAhern73
Instagram: @edwardahern1860
Twitter: @bottomstripper

FAMILY TREED

Too much knowledge can be upsetting.
Family records and lore tell me that I'm
half Irish, quartered English and Swedish.
To affirm provenance, I DNA tested.
The initial finding verified my beliefs,
but then they refined the results.
Much less Irish, English and Swedish
and big hunks of Welsh and Norwegian.
Who the hell were they?
And whose windows did they sneak through?

THE NAME CASCADE

The same names percolate through a family like a roof leak.
And except for the Juniors and Seniors no outsiders notice.

My mother's father was Edward Willman
He had five daughters, so his name died.
Almost.

After what I suspect was an argument,
My first and middle names became
Edward Willman.

I have a cousin whose middle name
Is also Willman, without Edward.
Probably a compromise.

Family memory seems to die away
In three modern generations
But I balked.

So our infant son was given
A middle name you'll guess.
A loving infliction.

Our son called when his son arrived.
And said the middle name was Willman.
The grandfathers are pleased.

LEGACY

The shuffling feet of those ahead
tramp a dust-clouded pathway
in which I just see and touch
the backs of those still living
and hear the wind-blown murmurs
of those gone further beyond.

The ever-fainter bobbing heads
have concocted my making
and conditioned my soul.
No matter how I turn
or twist away from them
their march is ever before me.

For will it or not
I am always of them,
Swaddled by ancestors
who mostly know me not,
staring ahead as they shuffle on,
never looking back.

Michael H. Brownstein

JEFFERSON CITY, MISSOURI

Michael's latest volumes of poetry, *A Slipknot to Somewhere Else* (2018) and *How Do We Create Love?* (2019), were published by Cholla Needles Press.

E: mhbrownstein@ymail.com

ON BECOMING - AN EVOLUTION

Rabbi Schwartz said, God is not dead,
but that was not my question.
I needed to know: *Why has God abandoned us?*
In response, I learned scripture,
segments of Torah, verses from the Old Testament.
I never received an answer.

Three decades later I wrote this:

"Let me start from the beginning:
Each one of us is responsible for our own actions,
not our parents no matter how abusive or evil,
not our teachers who may have bullied and insulted,
not our peers who showed us a code of behaviour we knew to be
wrong.
I was following orders is not an excuse."

A half decade later, this:

"Around the time Jews had already settled in Palestine (and many
other places), perhaps near the time of the grand Roman census or
centuries later, a man was about to be put to death. The rabbi who
was also the executioner asked if he had any last words. He nodded
his head toward the sea of onlookers. I'd like to whisper something to
my mother, he said. She's out there in the second row. His mother
was escorted to the platform and bent her ear to hear what her son
had to say. He bit it off. The rabbi aghast looked first to the mother
holding her hand to her head to stop the flow of blood and then to
her son who spit out the ear and calmly rubbed it into the wooden
platform. Why did you do that? The rabbi almost screamed. Calmly
the man answered, Since I was a small child, my mother taught me
only to do evil. This is why I am here today. The rabbi ran his fingers
through his beard. No, he said, that's not why. In your life journey,
you met many honest and good people and you - not because of your
mother - chose to ignore what they had to offer. Then the rabbi
pulled the lever and the man went to his death."

Then this happened:

I went to report on a poetry slam for a newspaper, was called an
anti-Semite because I was not supportive of Israel, and kicked out of
the venue before I even entered. *Can't stand Jews who hate Jews.* My

response: *I feel Israel is wrong many more times than it is right.* That does not make me less a Jew.

Conflicted.
Everything does not fall into order -
the sky fills itself with ash, the sea with plastic,
the clouds with a gray darkening,
and when the sun comes out,
a heart beats against the shadow of the palisades.

My writing is spiritual in nature, many times, abstract other times, and concrete still more times. I am a Jew who believes somewhere there is something that helps us want to do good. I believe there is a bit of God in all of us. I believe somehow humanity has lost its way, its taste, its ability to listen and its will. Nonetheless, I remain an eternal optimist.

Does my background enter into my writing. Maybe. Maybe not.

Carol Seitchik
BEVERLY, MASSACHUSETTS

Carol is the author of the poetry collection, *The Distance From Odessa*, published in January, 2021, (Atmosphere Press), and her poems have been published in the anthologies; *A Feast of Cape Ann Poets* (Folly Cove Press), *The Practicing Poet* (Terrapin Books), *Poetry Diversified: An Anthology of Human Experience* (Poetry Matters literary prize), *Tide Lines an anthology of Cape Ann Poets* (Rockport Press), and various other journals.
E: carolsei@comcast.net

SO MANY WORLDS

By the river, I watch a crow lift
one leg, balance on a small stump.
The breeze ruffles its black mantle.
Green parrots fly by in their frenzy,
like little bombers. One flies
into a small knothole in the tree.
Another tries to enter
but clearly there is no room.

That's how it is here — Other worlds
trying to live inside this world where history
grabs at the future, where the present
offers nothing unforgotten —

like Nazareth — ancient, biblical —
where I arrive at El Babour spice shop
on Annunciation Road, just past Mary's well
near the old Muslim cemetery.

So many claim this land. Who inherits
and what? Reality becomes inarticulate.

Each time, when I return home,
6,000 miles away, the question arises, always.
Will my daughter, now the Israeli, come back home?
I think about home, how it lands in me —
all that confusion, finding home.

But she has two small daughters and a husband,
born with the land in their breath.
They name it home, just like the mourning doves
perched by my window, dawn and dusk, chanting —
the way home can be so persistent.

SELFIE

Between myself and the camera,
there is endless discontent
as though my face, unruly in the moment,
teases me, as though something is left behind.
Wounds to heal.

What reveals is that space between my bones,
the quick pulse, the anchored skin,
the overcrowded interior hinting on the surface.

And if I look closely I can see
in my eyes that leftover guilt
from my unravelling mother —
a phone call last night,
feeling that quagmire
of adolescence seeping in.

How to retain the virtue of self.
I heard once that to create a work of art,
you remove the strongest formal element
to see how tough the rest of the composition is.

Click!

OF TWO WORLDS

A family story is often embellished
to maintain civility, to carry on
a bit of folklore, even myth. So much
culture is lost with my grandparents
who wanted only to tell stories forward.
What is behind is left behind —
waterlogged and underground.

I dig for childhood moments
from decades past, heartfelt moments
that sleep in the bones.
It's autumn and from my window
the scent of burning leaves —
like perfume from backyard Sundays —
the trashcan stuffed, flames flying skyward

and when I aim to dig deep,
I am looking for love to maintain a bond —
looking for the link of two worlds
so I confer with my parents long gone.
They're ethereal, even angel-like.
I long for them that way, to open the soul.
You wouldn't believe today, I tell them.

I tell them, life has become an art form —
what is left in these pandemic days is time.
I call it endurance-art, waiting-art,
what it means to live with uncertainty-art
and the challenge, to do it with aplomb,
to make sense of it all.

This early morning, I lean against the window —
a streak of light breaks through. Little moves.
The sun rises, the day becomes. One more.

Nolo Segundo
NEW JERSEY

Nolo Segundo is the pen name of L.J. Carber. Nolo only became a published poet as he neared his 8th decade, but has since had poems in published 35 literary magazines in the USA, UK, Canada, Romania, and India. In 2020, a trade publisher released a collection of his work titled *The Enormity Of Existence,* and in 2021 another collection titled *Of Earth and Earth*. Fifty years ago Nolo almost drowned in a Vermont river, and had a near-death experience which shattered his former faith in materialism; the idea that reality is only matter. He went from seeing life as meaningless, to knowing that the real problem was that there was so much meaning in everything - every action, every thought, every feeling. Being aware he has – is - a soul, an endless consciousness, may have helped him cope with teaching in the war zone of Cambodia, 1973-74 [leaving there about a year before the Killing Fields began]. He went on to teach ESL in Taiwan [where his wife is from] and Japan.
E: nolosegundo70@gmail.com

A CHILD'S CHRISTMAS CAROL

Then ... it was a time of true magic,
When the world was small and soft.
It had to be magic, my mind of five
Told me: how else could my brothers
And I go to sleep on an ordinary,
Dull and quiet night, to awaken in
Sheer joy the next morn as though
We had been zapped by a warm
Bolt of harmless lightning, setting
Our now restless bodies tingling ...

Like racehorses at the gate of magic,
We stood at the top of the stairs,
Pulling at whatever patience we
Could muster under the admonitions
Of Mom and Dad to wait! wait! the
Camera must be loaded—but how
Painful to be still when we knew
Children's paradise was only a
Stairway away—and what a
Paradise we saw unfolded in
Our now unfamiliar living room!

The tree drew our eyes first—
It was big and fat, with its
Branches sagging under all
Its myriad ornaments: glass
Balls, plastic candy canes,
Tinsel drooping as though
It hung on a weeping willow
And not a proud Blue Spruce.

And hundreds and millions of
Colored lights, some blinking,
Some staid, made our tree
Sparkle like the royal crown
Of a giant king—perhaps
The King of Toys, for they
Were seen in abundance
Wherever we looked: trucks
And bikes, and bats and games.
Each brother had his own pile

(we marvelled how thoughtful
Santa must be) and we knew
In each stack there were boxes
Beautifully wrapped but sans
Treasure, hiding only socks
Or shirts, perhaps a sweater.

Well, even the jolly fat man
Could not be perfect—still,
He would bring magic to our
Home every year, overnight
Transforming prosaic lives
By wonder, by magic, by love,
And after he went away,
When I was an ancient six,
The world grew much bigger
But colder, dull and empty
Of that special joy that
Can only come to those
Children who believe ...

Ruth Sabath Rosenthal
NEW YORK

Ruth is a New York City poet, well published in the U.S. And internationally. In October 2006, her poem *on yet another birthday* was nominated for a Pushcart prize by Ibbetson Street Press. Ruth has authored chapbook *Facing Home* published by Finishing Line Press and five full-length poetry books published by Paragon Poetry Press, Inc: *Of My Labor, Facing Home and beyond; little, but by no means small; Food: Nature vs Nurture; Gone, but Not Easily Forgotten*. Additionally, Ruth edited the autobiography *Manfred – His Story of Survival from Concentration Camp to Freedom in America*.
E: rsabathrosenthal@aol.com
W: newyorkcitypoet.com
W: bigapplepoet.com
W: www.poetrybyruthsabathrosenthal.com

DEEP IN THE YUGOSLAV MOUNTAINSIDE

in darkness but for slivers of moonlight
& bursts of floodlight i evade shoeless —
machine gun slung over one shoulder
& strapped across the other
a leather pouch holding coded messages
i deliver encampment to encampment —
locations i've been trained to find
in darkness & in rain & trained to focus on
blocking out thoughts of capture & torture —
me just a kid
escaped from a concentration camp
& rescued deep in the wilderness
by Tito's partisans
only to have them send me back
into that same mountainous terrain
night after night
unable to return to my farmhouse hideout
till i'd finished my courier rounds
night upon night
in the moments it takes me to
hang up my courier bag & machine gun
the fear that always nearly freezes me
begins melting away and i'm ready for my meal
of pit-roasted mutton & stone-ground bread
washed down with goat's milk —
that followed by a foot soak
(weekly a full-body scrub) then deep sleep
wrapped in some peasant women's hand-woven blankets
— my mattress — more blankets
placed on the cement floor of a dank cellar
hidden below an ordinary cellar
where night upon night
i get to dream of America

First published in *Of My Labor* (October 2021).

WHILE YOU WERE
After Leonard Cohen's "The Genius"

I was a daddy's little princess
having lots of wants and wishes
batting my eyelashes
my candy-coated coaxing
pursing my *M&M* sweetened lips
daddy always caving in muttering
something akin to "God help me" in Yiddish

a yeshiva boy
wearing a satin kippah my waking hours
and davening three times a day
knowing little of life outside my own
chowing down glatt pastrami on rye
kosher pickles & rugelach
Dr. Brown's Cel-Ray Tonic

a mommy's girl
mom not a *Rosie the Riveter*
hard at work for Uncle Sam
instead a real balabusta
with me her little clone
helping keep our kosher home ultra clean
our brisket & matzo balls truly kvell-worthy

a ghetto boy
surviving your thunderous reign
hiding my star and skull cap
sneaking out after curfew
foraging for anything to eat
walking not too quickly heart racing
focusing straight ahead sixth sense in high gear

First published in *Of My Labor* (October 2021).

WALTZ AFTER WALTZ

Inspired by Leonard Cohen's "Dance Me To the End of Love"

The four violinists, a truly scruffy blank-faced crew,
played on, they, key players in a role each of them knew
all too well. With eyes, no doubt, avoiding the blankness
in those in the mass of confusion of trembling nakedness
feet away, the musicians didn't miss a beat, as their brethren
were lining up for a "delousing" shower; You'll be given
clean blankets and new uniforms, and in a mess hall, fed
a hot meal and fresh water daily: this, a bit of what was read
them earlier, they couldn't have believed, not down deep
where terror must've been rising to the very brink of leap.
Though numb, they each shuffled along to the beat of a tune
not one of them had ever heard before — a particular tune
that endless more processions of such beleaguered souls, too,
shall hear, simply because each person processed was born a Jew.

First published in *Of My Labor* (October 2021).

Poet's Note: In a filmed interview of Leonard Cohen, shown in an extraordinary exhibit at The Jewish Museum in New York City, NY, April through September 2019: Leonard Cohen: A Crack in Everything. What Leonard Said (Paraphrased): The impetus for my poem "Dance Me To the End of Love" had nothing to do with "romantic" love or anything one would normally associate with "Love," but rather, how the Nazi SS routinely sought out musicians among the Jews in "extermination" camps, and had these musicians play during the process of their fellow- inmates being ushered into the gas chamber.

Darren B. Rankins
LAVERGNE, TENNESSEE

Darren began his writing career in sixth grade and became excited about poetry when the MTSU Honors Program Director suggested that Darren take part in the 1994 MTSU Poetry Slam. He has since had publications in several magazines and newspapers.
E: Purethoughts24@yahoo.com
W: www.purethoughts.info

THE AUTUMN LEAVES

that descend upon my heart
soon blanket the world with despair.
Free from compassion, love,
and forgiveness, a sweet goodbye.
A perfect picture of a darkened sky and
A graveyard of lost souls
without a way home.
Trying to distance myself
from the screams, crying, and pleading for the touch of another
heart.
Please tell me—without your love,
the touch of your hand,
and the sound of your voice,
I am lost deep
within the prison of my soul.

HOMELESS

Just drifting
Without money, food,
And a place to sleep.
Homeless is
The only name I have.

Gurupreet K. Khalsa
MOBILE, ALABAMA

Gurupreet holds a Ph.D. in Instructional Design. Her ancestors arrived in the US in 1640 on her mother's side from England, and her father's in 1711, from Swedish/German backgrounds. She taught middle and high-school English for many years, and is a part-time instructor in graduate education programs. Her work has appeared in *TL;DR Press, New York Quarterly, Far Side Review, Necro Productions, IHRAF Publishers, aurora journal, Last Leaves, Delta Poetry Review, Ricochet Review, Pure Slush*, and many others, and several of her poems have won awards.
E: gkhalsa@pacbell.net

CLAIMING NO ORIGIN

A family of twigs and sticks braided
in myriad tangled ways, branching
into colors, wraps rooty fingers
to hold deep in this new land.

Three hundred years on,
origins and tongues have drifted away
like migrant birds lost and blown
by winds they cannot see.

American is left,
suitcases of heritage long forgotten
in the journey's stations.
What is origin? Mine, none.

Pinny Bulman
THE BRONX, NEW YORK

Pinny was raised in a shrinking Jewish community within the Washington Heights neighbourhood of New York. He is a Bronx Council on the Arts BRIO award-winning poet (2014). He has also been winner of the Poets of NYC Contest, recipient of several ADR Poetry Awards, and a finalist for the Raynes Poetry Prize. His poems recently appeared in the anthologies *Undeniable* (Alternating Current Press) and *Escape Wheel* (great weather for MEDIA) and were published in Korean translation for *Bridging the Waters III* (Korean Expatriate Literature & Cross-Cultural Communications). Pinny's poetry has also appeared or is upcoming in a variety of other literary publications including: *The London Reader, Muddy River Poetry Review, Artemis, Pressenza International, Red Paint Hill*, and *Poetry Quarterly.*
E: pinnybulman@gmail.com

SWASTIKA

as graffiti it wasn't
much to look at
a few crude lines in marker
down a flight of side stairs
on the door of the shul's emergency exit
almost hidden amidst the other usual tags

nothing like the nearby mural
a half-block explosion of swirling colorful pain
depicting presidential patriarchs found on paper money
exploring their role as slaveowners
perpetuating the country's economy of racism,
all this on the side of a bank

but it was the small anonymous nazi pinwheel
that pushed me to action
to go out that night armed
with a black sharpie,
squeeze through the bent bars
of the locked side gate to
blot out the swastika
mark up the area with jewish stars
my own ancient tag

soon after,
the shul door was repainted
the mural wall whitewashed

in fact it's been years since that bank
was torn down
the shul soon to follow,
and when i die
the only thing standing between
that swastika and complete oblivion
will be this poem

but i am of a people who understand
the importance of tagging history,
keeping a memory of all that needs
to be erased.

JERUSALEM

the huge stones of these
ancient prayer spaces
press down heavily with
the weight of forgotten sacrifice,
worship measured in millennium
interrupted by
the occasional sabbatical centuries
the groaning relief of exile,
to these places
the dead shul across
the ocean barely existed
a hundred-year-old fruit fly

according to tradition
a newborn who dies
is like a stillbirth
the mourner's kaddish is not said,
but i will not be silenced
my prayer will echo
off these indifferent stones
if only for
a moment.

FACING WEST

we prayed facing west,
at our backs
a crowded history
occasionally coughing apologetically
asking for the page number

and in front
high above the ark
a series of twelve
stained glass square panels
neither tribes nor prophets

an exile's vision
of promised land as
otherworldly landscape
curving shapes
in shades of crimson violet
a messianic dream of quiet abstraction
several panels hinting
at an ancient city
distant enough to render
questions of habitation
nationality religion
irrelevant

but when shabbos exhaled
sun setting behind the neighbouring apartment building
the darkness that fell across the twelve panels
was a hebrew darkness
moving from right to
left in a language of gentle erasure
until the moment when
nothing left to see
we turned east
and exited the shul
into night.

Robert Beveridge

AKRON, OHIO

Robert has had poetry published, or forthcoming in *Ephemeral Elegies, Pulsebeat*, and *Riverbed Review*, among others.
E: xterminal@gmail.com
W: www.xterminal.bandcamp.com
Instagram: @ebolaisthesavior

BONNEVILLE

The Furry convention picked the salt flats
for their annual gathering. Panthers, lynx,
wolves on two legs converge, skintight
spandex, cleavage in abundance. This zoo
is all about the petting, but the wristband
is dear.

       There are medals to be won
in enough categories to make the sponsors
sit up and take notice. Chinese puzzle-box
solving? If only one could draw a paycheck!
Instead, though, the sea emperor comes
to call, picks up your successes, transports
them to the Hall of Fame on errant waves.
Leaves you trying to figure out if your gold
goes better with the rabbit costume or the fox.

There's pony trouble in the saloon, two moose
in fisticuffs at the licks. Early reports say box-
office receipts are up twenty-four percent;
rumor has it the stuffed shirts and talking heads
debate even as we speak about whether
the relaxation of the liquor ordinance is justified.
The line outside the movie house is long,
and long, even if no one knows what's queued.
Surprise is inevitable, and the back row
remains reserved for spider cosplay
and smiles that cannot, cannot be human.

HOME SHOW

and you wake up and are
in the mood for a chickenskin
hot dog with walnut relish
and Louisiana fire ant slaw

and you get to the shop
and place your order and they
won't stop their Peabo Bryson
marathon (you're okay
with Peabo Bryson, but not
eight hours' worth)

and when you ask for the Wi-Fi
password they tell you that today
it's Crosswinds and you just
shake your head and sit down

and take a bite and that slaw
stings just the way you hoped

and you fire up Google Maps
like you do every single day
and you search street view
for pizza delivery guys who
look as if they might be
that one who mugged your
brother Robert back in 1984
and then framed him for that
big game hunting debacle
that still besmirches his name

and your mind wanders to whether
you can get this dog with added
pepperoni while you notice
that this house in Jengre has
the most interesting Tudor style

MARUTA

The woodcutter gathers
fuel. Each log resembles
a dead countryman.

The closer he gets
to Harbin, the more
loath he is to burn
his spoils.

Last night, in a hollow,
he discovered
a gold tooth,
a broken wristwatch,
cracked, yet still
ticking.

Peter David Goodwin
NORTH EAST, MARYLAND

Raised in England, Peter moved back to USA at age 18 in pursuit of an egalitarian education. Eventually settling in New York City, he worked in a variety of occupations while indulging his love for theatre and relishing the city's vibrant chaos. But starved for light, he removed himself to the Chesapeake Bay, appreciating its natural rhythms and slower seasons.
E: peterdgoodwin@me.com
W: www.peterdgoodwin.net

THE ANCESTORS

Are they talking about me, muttering, clicking
their tongues, sighing—those ancestors of mine
generations of the distinguished, my successful
family, generations who built business, in good times
and bad, from a rented flour mill on a small dammed
river to prosperous businesses in large cities, generations
creating family wealth, comfort, and prestige, and I
was to continue that tradition.

Even as a small boy I knew it—
the obligation, the necessity, the burden.
I saw them proud, their portraits, their marble
busts, the solid polished furniture, the gleaming
silverware, the inscribed tray by the front entrance,
used for the mail, the silver platters on the sideboard,
even at breakfast, keeping warm the scrambled eggs,
the bacon and sausage, sometimes kippers, the silver
bowls for sugar, salt, pepper and mustard; all around
me I was surrounded by the work of my ancestors,
and the garden with never an unsightly weed,
and the lawn close cropped, smooth and soft
and beyond the garden wall—a land un-manicured,
rough, disorganized, while inside an air of distance
and disapproval—with the changing world and
with me as I proved to be a poor athlete and an
undistinguished student lacking our traditional
self discipline, a day dreamer

while I dreamed that one day
I would make my ancestors
proud and soon ...

I must face them.

IN OUR NEIGHBOURHOOD, SHE DID NOT BELONG

With her dark complexion she stood apart
this gypsy woman in her bright colors
her very black hair, peddling wooden
clothes pegs, which my mother always bought
whether she needed them or not.

On the side of the road I often saw their wooden
wagons so foreign with their bright painted colors,
their patient horses, and their small children not
dressed properly, their life on display not hidden
behind walls and fences, and when I passed by
on my bike I always peddled fast, we knew
all about those thieving gypsies, we knew
to be suspicious of anyone with dark
dangerous skin, who did not dress normally,
who led unsettled lives and we knew to treat
them with extreme caution, this was in the days
when the world was right, there was no crime,
all was peaceful, we all had pale skins,
knew right from wrong, what
was proper and what wasn't.

No, that is not exactly true.
There was an Irish boy in the neighbourhood
and we were warned not to play
with him, and usually we didn't and
if we did it usually ended badly.
He was somewhat swarthy, too
which perhaps explained a lot.
The Irish were also strangers and did not belong
so we learned to be wary of them as well. but—
on the whole we led a perfectly peaceful life, but—

no one warned me
about the bigger kids who were bullies,
friends who were fickle
families who were ferocious
love that could be lacerating
no one warned me about our neighbours
who were often nasty
or sweet and scolding
no one warned me

that the world could be cruel
no one warned of
the dangers lurking
in the normal and the familiar
I only worried about the strangers
the gypsies who did not belong
who suddenly appeared
and just as suddenly disappeared
who led free, unpredictable lives
who could not be trusted ...

now, when I think back
to my old neighbourhood
I cannot remember my friends
who were bullies or fickle
the neighbours who were sweet or nasty
but I do remember
the gypsies with their bright bold colors

who are no more.

Antoni Ooto
NEW YORK

Antoni is an internationally published poet and flash fiction writer, as well as being well-known for his abstract expressionist art. He now adds his voice to poetry; reading and studying the works of many poets has opened another means of self-expression. His recent poems have been published in *Amethyst Review, The BeZine, The Poet Magazine, The Active Muse, The Wild Word*, and a number of journals and anthologies.
E: antoniotoart@gmail.com
W: www.ooto.org
LinkedIn: @antoniooto

IGLESIA
1953

no one sweeping the stairs
       no one comes and goes
           no posted services
a soundless congregation

     (curious thoughts of a young child)

this small chapel lacking sacramental staging
alongside the butcher
more a landscape where people passed by…
heard little…saw no one
on this German-Irish-Italian block

Dutchtown's misplaced immigrant
foreign, mysterious marking time
in silence …
curious

Previously published by *Amethyst Review*, September 2018

GARLIC

For Giovannina DeCroce, grandmother.

Next to oxygen, it was a life force,
the first thing you'd smell
at 49 Lime Street.

Depending on time or season,
windows open or shut,
rooms had it by degrees.

Used for cooking,
for protection against the "Malocchio."
and as a medicinal supplement ...

Giovannina ground it fine
mixing it with olive oil and black pepper--
dipped her finger in
and swabbed my sore throat.

Rocking## me asleep
neen na naw, neen na naw.
singing her lullaby
            with the taste of garlic.

HOMETOWN

On these streets, new families
live behind those same fragile doors.

In tight rows of houses
where immigrants once settled from Lithuania/Poland.

St Casmir's steeple arrows over the Mohawk,
anchoring that neighbourhood where mills still flourished

both before and after the wars.
Amsterdam, New York, a city, now stalled in rust.

Yet, in what remains of a church parking lot,
Asian children surround a teacher.

Standing nearby,
a handmade replica of Liberty,

and at her feet, a wooden plaque
with characters in Korean/Chinese.

Published previously by *The Electric Rail*, January 2021.

Judy DeCroce
NEW YORK

Judy lives and works with her husband poet/artist Antoni Ooto in rural upstate New York. Widely published internationally in print, online journals, and anthologies, she is a poet, flash fiction writer, and educator who is a regular contributor to *The BeZINE, The Front Porch Review, North of Oxford, OpenDoor Magazine, The Poet Magazine, Amethyst Review*, and *Vita Brevis Press*. Judy is proud of being invited, for a second year, to participate in the Waco Wordfest Oct. 2021. As a professional storyteller, she enjoys preforming and teaching that genre.
E: judydecroce@yahoo.com
LinkedIn: @JudyDeCroce

A LOUD CACOPHONY

The world is too loud for angels
        I recall the quiet of churches
                the precipice of curbs

the spokey sound of bikes
        voices calling friend to friend,
                mom to home,

a parenthesis of quiet
        trying to poke through
                trucks, trains, a fading clatter

now noise moves around
        through
                and around again

carried in pockets
        n hands
                in clouds ... somehow.

Previously published by *Amethyst Review*, September 2019.

Mark Fleisher

ALBUQUERQUE, NEW MEXICO

Mark's writings have taken him around the world – his work has been published in numerous online and print anthologies in the United States, United Kingdom, Canada, Nigeria, Kenya, South Africa, and India. He has also published three volumes of poetry – with prose and photography added - titled *Moments of Time, Intersections: Poems from the Crossroads* and *Reflections: Soundings From the Deep*, and has collaborated on a fourth book *Obituaries of the Living*. Fleisher received a journalism degree from Ohio University. His service in the United States Air Force included a year as a combat news reporter in Vietnam, where he was awarded a Bronze Star for meritorious service.

E: markfleisher111@gmail.com
E: markfleisher333@gmail.com

WE ARE OURSELVES

A summer afternoon
in the Plaza approached
by a camera-toting tourist
Are you Native American?
no, I politely reply
Are you Hispanic?
Again, my answer is no

If I had said yes
to either question would
she want to take my picture?
Would I have been something
of an oddity to her very whiteness?

And so the identity game is played
by searching for a slot,
a niche, pigeon-holed
by ourselves or strangers
Am I not to be considered
an individual person
whether brown, black, white
whether Jew, Christian,
Muslim, Buddhist, atheist?

Did not a wise and thoughtful
man advise us to judge
one another by the content
of our character?

Let me tell you who I am

I am a complexity, a contradiction, a complication
I am your daily planner
I am spontaneously combusted by existential forces
I am a risk taker, courting catastrophe
I am unafraid to disconnect from the know
I am unafraid of unfamiliar landscapes
I am shielded from the curious by panes thick with frost
I am entered by the chosen through permitted transparencies
I am witness to the sting of tumultuous death
I am mindful of a quiet passing
I am mourning all in God's design

I am a minnow in a school of swimmers speaking alien languages
I am walking only in my tracks
I am No Man
I am Every Man.

Sunayna Pal
MARYLAND

Born and raised in Mumbai, India, poet Sunayna now happily resides in Maryland with her husband, children, plants and an invincible goldfish. Holding degrees from XLRI and Annamalai University, Sunayna's poetry is published extensively in international journals and anthologies, with recent credits in *Subterranean Blue Poetry, Cecile's Writers*, and *Poetry Super Highway*. Sunayna is also working on a collection of poetry on the Partition and Sindh.
E: sunayna.pal@gmail.com
W: www.sunaynapal.com
FB: @LearningAboutSindh

IDENTITIES

I've had many.

Daughter
Student
Teacher
Wife
Mother.

Never did I realize,
I am also a granddaughter
         of a refugee.

CHOICES

Some chose riots and curfews
rearranging the peace.

Some chose fish and bones
violating their *hawans*.

Some chose hiding behind *boris*
only to be stabbed through the wheat
but not allowed to wince.

Some chose daughters being kidnapped
from *mandaps* and married off to old men.

Some chose death
as they refused to leave
the soil on which they were born.

NOTE:
Havan - holy ritual which gets impurified with fish.
Mandap - holy place for Indian marriages.
Boris - Sack of produce or grains.

INCOMPLETE
A memory uncertain about a sentence - Kimberly Alidio

Along with bedtime stories my grandma told me
she shared stories of living and then leaving
the only home she ever knew.

While feeding me the bitter sai bhaji
she told me to eat well and healthy
for one never knows life.

She shared memories
that only left her eyes
but never crossed her obedient tongue

With rice and bhaji in her hand
her mind on the pain of partition
which I never understood ...

Margaret Duda
STATE COLLEGE, PENNSYLVANIA

Margaret is the daughter of Hungarian immigrants. She has had her work published in the *Kansas Quarterly, the Michigan Quarterly Review*, the *South Carolina Review, Crosscurrents, The Green River Review, Fine Art Discovery, Venture, Silver Birch Press*, and *Around the World: Landscapes and Cityscapes*. She writes poetry, short stories, non-fiction, and is working on the final draft of a novel. One of her short stories made the list of Best American Short Stories.
E: mduda@ceinetworks.com

THE FRAGILITY OF FILM

I always knew I had a brother named Jozsef,
although Papa told me I could call him Joey.
He was from the first reel of Papa's life
captured in eight millimetres of silence.

To avoid being drafted by the Romanians
who were awarded his part of Hungary,
Papa joined his older brother in America,
to be followed by his wife after Joey was born.

But Kati died in a long and difficult childbirth,
leaving Joey to be raised by her parents
in a section of Hungary, now Romania,
which tried to expunge the Magyar culture
by changing the names of people and places.

Mama and I were from the second reel,
set in America between the Depression,
World War Two, and the Iron curtain era,
long after talkies and theatres were invented.

Joey's moustached, uniformed image framed
on my nightstand kept him in my thoughts.
I talked to Joey, prayed for Joey, and loved him
with all my heart, as only a seven year old can.

Unlike Papa, Joey was drafted in World War 2
by Romanians who mistreated Magyar conscripts.
Papa decided to help Joey escape to America
but had to secretly send him money for bribes.

Used garments made it through inspections,
so like the director a movie, Mama bought
tattered items of clothing at the Goodwill store
and sewed money into an old overcoat lining.

Papa sent the package to his sister, also caught
in the blurry existence of Magyars in Romania.
She tore open the living, gingerly removing bills
as Mama instructed. All we had left to do was pray.

We repeated the same prayers over and over

as if memorizing an actor's dialogue while
Papa anxiously awaited Joey's appearance
as one awaits the opening scene of a movie.

A letter finally arrived from Papa's sister,
telling us Joey was captured at the border
and incarcerated for five years in a prison
in Romania or Russia. No one knew where.

Papa was inconsolable, crying every night,
Our life was never the same. After his release,
Joey married, had a son, and sent photos,
but never again tried to escape to America.11Q.

Joey died at fifty, leaving a wife and teenaged son
who spoke only Romanian we did not understand.
It was as if the film of Joey's existence had expired,
along with his last name, leaving only fading images
of a brother I never met, but continued to love.

A MOTHER'S COURAGE

What gave you the courage
to leave a foster mother who loved you
and cross an ocean on a grand ship
to come to a mother you never met?

What gave you the courage
to leave a cruel stepfather
and become a governess
when you didn't even speak English?

What gave you the courage
to marry a man you met on a
Hungarian dinner-dance cruise
and start a new life together?

What gave you the courage
to get pregnant and give birth to me
after you'd already had one miscarriage
and were told not to try again?

What gave you the courage
with only six years of schooling
to take me to the library every week
and teach me to love books as you did?

What gave you the courage
to listen when my third grade teacher
told you I had to go to a place called college
to make sure you saved for my tuition?

What gave you the courage
to clean houses after Papa's heart attack,
then decide you could do better and open
a small Hungarian restaurant?

What gave you the courage
after reading my first short story
to buy me a used typewriter
and tell me to follow my heart?

What gave you the courage
to see that writing made me happy

and was the reason I was put on earth
to give me the chances you never had?

Lou Faber
COCONUT CREEK, FLORIDA

Louis is a poet, amateur photographer and blogger. He is a retired Corporate Attorney and College English Literature Adjunct Professor. Adopted at birth, he has searched for his origins and only found them thanks to DNA testing. He found his birth parents after they had died, but he found his heritage as well, not what he expected, all that he had hoped. His roots come from Lithuania, Ireland, Scotland, England, Norway, France and Wales and his ancestors were a polyglot of faiths, saints, kings and sinners. His work has appeared in *Dreich (Scotland), Tomorrow and Tomorrow, Erothanatos, Defenestration, Atlanta Review, Glimpse, Rattle, Cold Mountain Review, Eureka Literary Magazine, Borderlands: the Texas Poetry Review, Midnight Mind, Pearl, Midstream, European Judaism, The South Carolina Review* and *Worcester Review*, among many others, and in online journals in India, China, Ireland, Pakistan and elsewhere, and has been nominated for a Pushcart Prize. A book of poetry, *The Right to Depart*, was published by Plain View Press.
E: lfaberfl@outlook.com
W: www.anoldwriter.com
W: www.bird-of-the-day.com

A PERFECT STILLNESS

You lie there, perfectly still,
the morning breeze slides away
leaving the sun to stare down,
and the birds fall into silence.

I gently touch the stone, feel
your cheek beneath my finger,
see your face, the college yearbook
photo all that I have of you.

I speak silently to you, telling
of my sixty-seven years, of your
grandsons and great grandchildren
and I sense your smile, and a tear.

Your parents are here, your
grandparents, sisters, brothers
and cousins, and I know give
you three generations more.

It is time for me to go, but these
moments are the most I have
of you, and as I place my small stone
atop yours, I now have a mother.

TO PROTECT THE INNOCENT

I am there, a classroom,
elementary or middle school,
Charleston, West Virginia
1930's, girls in proper skirts,
saddle shoes, the old woman
at the front of the room,
first day of a new year.

"Jones", a hand goes up,
"Murphy", another rises slowly,
"Padlibsky, what kind
of name is that, Jew, or
some kind or Ruskie maybe?"
A small voice answers
Lithuanian, ma'am.

A scene that never
happened, a name changed
so that day the teacher
called out "Wells"
and she smiled and
quickly raised her hand.

THIS LAND IS WAS MY LAND

I would very much like
to look down from above,
unseen by those below,
on my country, see the turmoil
roiling so many, the lines
formed at borders, a queue
for those deemed less valuable,
and I wonder where in the line
my ancestors would be
were they still alive.
I wonder what life
would be like if I
was born in Lithuania
or if my parents never met.
I wonder, too, what life
would be like if we still
honoured the principles
our ancestors came here to find.

Timothy Resau

BALIMORE, MARYLAND

Timothy's poems and prose have recently appeared in *The Sparrow's Trombone, Sylvia Magazine, The Beautiful Space, Loch Raven Review, Babel Tower Notice Board, Better than Starbucks, Fictional Café, BlazeVOX, Ephemeral Elegies, The Metaworker, KGB Bar Literary Journal*, and is forthcoming in *Superpresent, New Note Poetry, Soul-Lit,* and *Poetica*.

E: timwresau@gmail.com

LONDON, NIGHT, & RAIN

Two visions of night—
obscure as a fingerprint, a message of mercy—
Outside the leaden-glass windows, the cold rain falls—

Gray day, damp London—

We protect our weary hearts and souls,
saying a saviour approaches,
shall ascend—
Those chosen to wait remain,
drinking the sacred wine from bent chalices ...
prancing about our crescent alters—
we, the hopeful, chant Hindu hymns,
beating our thin thumbs against tiny tin drums.

Gray day, damp London—

Waiting in this faith-filled stupor,
some clap leather bound hands, watching
our disappointing game of chess with shadows—
amid the frost of time, and now our chairs no longer
fit comfortably about our backs—
we serve no purpose—
Whimper night while we pack pieces of
ourselves into the glass suitcases we'll leave behind.

THE FALL

Strange breezes blow down these city alleyways,
crossing the mind's back streets,
like a child pushing a wagon full of memories
through a neighbour's uneven yard.

Be careful ... be ever so careful ...

All those lost neighbourhood names:
from a long-a-go city, *Baltimore*:
Edmonson Avenue,
          Prospect Avenue,
                    Dunmore Road ...
                              & Old Frederick Road—

The pencilled faces of *Crazy Ernie*,
Sonny Gentile, Donny Cornet, & Jimmy Connelly—
Susan Thomson, & dear Buddy Harper—
gifted, & cherished as big sister's call ...
 "Timothy",
which never came—

A mother's special kiss ... arriving too late—
A neighbour's humble blush ...
a recent forgotten charcoal sketch—

Sudden thoughts that tend to fade, like Mary's yellow hair,
and reappear—*Mary's here*—and repeat like names in the street.

Be careful ... be ever so careful ...

GILBERT, THE ACTOR

He bends, elastic as he is, bearing vocal cuts and scarlet wounds.
Strength, he says: — pulls the voices across my life. All my
adventures have ended upon the formulated stage, not upon
mountains—
A life of illusion and nightmares, portrayed by Gilbert, the actor, sell
well in
the poor sections of our wealthy cities.

Behind the floodlights he wears masks to cover his face,
cufflinks upon his tailored shirts, and he dyes his hair for each new
part—
it's his eyes he cannot hide.
Alone, upon the alter of his soul, he weeps, clutching his matinee
idol's head
in a *Cinemascope* attempt to stop the pain—

Socially, he dines with friends, using his Shakespearean voice,
counting on their laughter to bath his wounds.
Then, early in the morning, he pardons himself—
feeling naked in evening dress — and goes to bed,
a sinner kneeling in his own sin — a mere reflection, frozen
mechanically,
like each of the personal photos on his wall.

Neal Whitman

PACIFIC GROVE, CALIFORNIA

Neal is an award-winning member of both the Californian Federation of Chaparral Poets, and the Ina Coolbrith Circle that celebrates the legacy of its namesake, a pioneering woman in early 20th century Bohemian literature and art. In 2021, one of Neal's poems was awarded and recited at the annual Amici di Guido Zozzano in Agié, Italy, and won Best Foreign Poem in Italy's Il Colori Dell'Anima (The Colors of the Soul). Incised on a granite stone on the path to their front door are the words of Henry David Thoreau: *ex orient lux / ex occident frux.*

E: neal.pgpoet@gmail.com
W: www.poetryfoundation.org/poets/neal-whitman-5e94cf6ed5cd6

HOW MAD IS THIS?

The British put in internment camps
German nationals in India.
A fellow inmate
tells a Jewish family:
"Rommel's coming to save us,
but not you."
Is this madness?
In his painting, Birth of a New World,
Salvador Dali teaches us
that the only difference
between a mad man and himself
is that he was not mad.

Wilda Morris
BOLINGBROOK, ILLINOIS

Wilda is a widely-published poet who has won awards for free and formal verse and haiku. She is a former president of the Illinois State Poetry Society and currently serves a workshop chairperson for Poets & Patrons of Chicago. Her latest book is *Pequod Poems: Gamming with Moby-Dick* (Kelsay, 2019). One of Wilda's ancestors was tarred and feathered and driven out of a Kentucky town when he left the Catholic priesthood, married, and became a Free Will Baptist preacher. About a century later, Wilda's mother patched up the relationship between the Catholic and Protestant branches of the family tree, and and discovered much of their diverse, though mostly European-American, ancestry. Wilda finds it difficult to claim her cultural heritage - or rather cultural heritages - because she is a mixture of Dutch, Flemish, French Huguenot, Scottish, Scots-Irish, Irish, English, German, and, according to family tradition, Native American.

E: wem@ameritech.net
W: www.wildamorris.blogspot.com

PONDERING MY ROOTS

Grandmother says we are part American Indian,
so I ask if our ancestors were among the Cayuga
who welcomed the forebears of Europeans who later
drove them from New York.

Did they come from the Iroquois who taught federalism
to Ben Franklin? Or the Cherokee who built villages
along streams of Appalachia, till Andrew Jackson, whose life
had been saved by a Cherokee, sent them on the Trail of Tears?

Am I cousin to Cheyenne massacred at Sand Creek?
Or the Ottawa who were given smallpox-infected blankets?
Am I part Apache? Hopi? Algonquian? Sioux?
Grandmother does not know.

I like to think I'm kin to the Blackfoot brave
who defined life as *the flash of a firefly in the night,*
the breath of a buffalo in the winter time, the little shadow
which runs across the grass and loses itself in the sunset.

When my little shadow has vanished,
will I know, at last, this part of who I am?

IN AMSTERDAM

I step into the sanctuary of the Nieuwe Kerk, eager
to hear a concert played on the pipe organ built
by Hans Wolff Schonat in 1655, not the same organ
my ancestors Cornelius and Jennekin Melyn heard—
they'd already left for the new world in 1641—
but the same building where they worshipped
and brought their older children to be baptized.

As I listen to Bach, I imagine them walking in,
Cornelius carries my eighth great-grandmother.
I imagine Jennekin dressed like the woman with the balance
in Vermeer's painting. She wears a white veil
over dark hair. Her blue jacket is trimmed with white.

I ponder if her life was as balanced as the painting,
as orderly and harmonic as the music pouring
from the organ. What was the true timbre
of her days? Torn from the city of her birth,
taken with her children to New Amsterdam,
a city not ready for pipe-organs or art galleries.

How did she adjust the stops created
by this counterpoint to the life she knew?
How did she maintain composure as her husband
feuded with the governor? How would Vermeer
have painted her when someone came
to tell her how her son drowned?

As I listen to the music of the pipe organ,
I can't help painting pictures in my mind,
can't help wishing I knew more
of my Dutch ancestors.

THE MIDWIFE OF POITOU, FRANCE, 1635
For my nephews and nieces

Louis XIII sits dressed in velvet and crown,
but Cardinal Richelieu rules, drives Huguenots
from their homes, raises taxes to pay for wars,
palaces and châteaus for himself, dances
and banquets at court. Peasants pommel
and bludgeon each other for a few crumbs of bread.

The midwife who picks up the child, slaps life
into his lungs, does not know how much depends
on this babe forced from the warm comfort
of the womb; doesn't know he—with his father's name
and his Mother's eyes—one day will turn his back
on France and search for a new life in another land.
She doesn't know he will tire of tossing waves,
sigh with relief when at last he sets his feet
on the motionless soil of Staten Island.

The midwife cannot picture you careening
down a snow-covered hill in your blue jacket,
your gloved hands holding the toboggan rope.
She doesn't know without him, you would never
be born. She dips the cloth in warm water,
wipes afterbirth from your eighth great-grandfather,
wraps him in blankets, lays him, still birth-blind,
in his mother's welcoming arms.

Djehane Hassouna
PITTSBURGH, PENNSYLVANIA

Growing up a few steps away from the Egyptian pyramids and the mysterious world of the pharaohs, Djehane received her BA in French, her MA in Comparative Literature, and, at 62 years old, earned her PhD in Romance Languages and Literatures. Despite her struggle with Parkinson's disease, at the age of 76, she also published her first book of poetry, *Rainbow of Emotions*. Djehane is multicultural and speaks five languages: French, English, Arabic, Italian, and Spanish. Her creativity knows no bounds, and plans to continue writing poems, as well as publishing many more books.

E:djehane@gmail.com

W: www.djehane-poetry.com

FB: @DjehanePoetry

Instagram:@ DjehanePoetry

Twitter:@DjehanePoetry

Goodreads: @20994286.Djehane_Hassouna

Allpoetry.com: @DjehanePoetry

LINEAGE

As a child, my next-door neighbours were the pharaohs of
Ancient Egypt who left their mark on
The whole Egyptian landscape!
On this spot, the monuments built by the three Kings:
Cheops, Kefren, and Mykerinos stood tall, magnificent, and
Indestructible. Built of huge blocks of stone,
The apex topped with granite,
The pyramids fascinated tourists and were
The ideal destination for camel drivers and horsemen to take
Their riders! When people reached the plateau
Of Giza overlooking the city of Cairo,
They were not only spectators, but also
Witnesses to the legacy of past centuries.
Although modern bystanders, they, somehow, participated
In the exceptional life of the ancient Egyptians.
They glimpsed at their glory, at such a mysterious way of life,
At their extraordinary mausoleums reaching the sunny sky
Of the Egyptian desert... How fortunate was I to have such
Glorious neighbours, whose distinguished civilization
Kept my young imagination relentlessly engaged!
Who knows? King Tut, the Boy King, could possibly
Have been a distant relative of mine!

First published in *Rainbow of Emotions.*

A WITNESS TO ETERNITY

The Great Sphinx crouches on the desert sand,
Fastening his gaze on a mysterious hereafter.
A witness to Eternity, he appears to be
Indifferent to the Present, like Napoleon,
Obsessed with the past glory of his era;
His sole vision is a Future he is able to predict.
Walled in an immutable silence, keeping the secrets
Of Time and Space as well as Eternal Memory,
His granite eyes can pierce the walls of the Unknown.
Exposed to the elements for four thousand years,
Oblivious to the devastating effect of aging, and
The constant erosion of Time gnawing at his features,
He patiently bears his Fate. Mute, magnanimous,
Insightful, and apathetic, he watches the human circus
Proceed and unfold in a ludicrous minuet,
As people make fools of themselves...

First published in *Rainbow of Emotions*.

CHILD OF THE DESERT

My identity was shaped by two cultures:
The culture of the desert, and the culture of enlightenment.

My demanding parents and my exigent grandmother,
Enforced the rules of the desert.
I kept wishing for a time when I was not expected to obey.
It is so unfair to feel that you were created to follow injunctions.
When will you be allowed to explore your own ideas, to have your
own feelings,
To follow your own directions, to find your purpose in life.

My grandfather offered me a window of enlightenment,
He was the only one who trusted my judgment.
He considered me to be smart, confident,
Sure of myself, of my wishes and desires.
I felt better talking to him, walking with him,
Listening to him and learning from him.
I trusted him as much as he trusted me.
Together, we experienced the Egyptian civilization
As well as the European ones!

In my struggle for identity, I was caught between
My grandmother's traditional views and
My grandfather's open-mindedness.
In my desire for freedom, my identity will be forever multicultural …

Karen Douglass
COLORADO

Karen is a native New Englander, but now lives in Colorado. She has been a psychiatric nurse, horsewoman, racetrack judge, mother (still is), college instructor, poet, and novelist.
E: kvdbooks@gmail.com

CITY LIFE

As a sidewalk artist
I could chalk a ripening apple
on gray cement. First, I make
an imperfect outline.

I'm new at this, but let's say
I draw a good-enough apple,
but big, four or five feet across,
filling the walkway. Next
I add a stem and one leaf,
color the stem true brown.
The leaf, because it's art, is blue.
Then fill in the pome, pale green
with a blush of red on the shoulder.
There, done.

Pedestrians skirt the apple.
A hairy dog dragging its leash
scratches the apple skin,
releasing into the air apple essence.
Then rain takes a bite,
colors run, no more apple, just
wet chalk gracing the gutter.

HOMELESS

Give me a cup and fill me.
Swaddled in rags, I forage
in dreary weather.
I pack myself in canvas,
a carry-on bag for life,
what's left of it. Grind

my bones to make my bread,
flat as folding one. Life
comes down to a hug of fabric
and how not to be alone with

empty hands. Who isn't naked,
left alone on the doorstep
of an abandoned monastery?

SCATTERING GRATITUDE

Prying it out of another day
like digging a root crop
buried deep—beets, yams maybe—

like a field worker, though my hands
stay clean and uncallused as I work
to harvest thanks enough to share,

one for the diner cook, unseen,
who flips my eggs just in time.
And for that warehouse crew

who pack, label, load my order,
I'll fling a little gratitude around
like seed in the poultry yard,

scratch the ground of my grubby life
hoping to share one more thank you
before the fox comes for me.

Laura Blatt

PENNGROVE, CALIFORNIA

Now retired, Laura has worked as a website writer, a laboratory technician and a publishing company manager. Her writing has appeared in *The Poet, Thema, Lilith Magazine, California Quarterly,* and several poetry anthologies.

E: laurahikes@icloud.com

PURIM FESTIVAL

Disguised as Superman
the rabbi leaps from a table
piled with fresh-baked hamantaschen
lands near Queen Esther,
a little girl in long pink gown
and high heels she cannot yet fill.

Esther joins
the children's costume parade
lion
tiger
Haman,
may he be cursed.

Metallic noise of groggers
blot out Haman's name
but betrayal
cannot be concealed
even by a three-cornered hat
filled with prunes and dates.

A woman once came to our rescue
hidden as an obedient wife
but bolder than silence.
We shout her name—Esther—
to call back her spirit
for one day of divine revelry.

A DAY OF REST

Begin at sunset
with challah and candles
dinner for two or more
praise on printed pages
a book of poems.

Turn off
phones
computers
all electronics.
Turn up inner voice.

At sunrise enjoy
luscious strawberries
so sweet
so fragrant
in oatmeal with cream.

With sunshine and curiosity
observe the Goddess of
creeks and ferns
connect with heart
arrive at yet another sunset.

First published in *Phoenix*, Redwood Writers 2018 poetry anthology.

Alexis Garcia
NEW YORK

Alexis is a queer Hispanic writer from New York. She graduated from Manhattanville College in 2017, where she studied Creative Writing and Criminal Law. Currently, she works as a paralegal at a personal injury law firm. A few of her poems have been published in the anthologies *UNITED: Volume RED* and *UNITED: Volume HONEY* with Beautiful Minds Unite LLC, and *Upon Arrival: Threshold* with Eber & Wein Publishing. She has had more of her poems accepted for publication in *Ariel Chart, Third Estate Art, Door is a Jar, Mixed Mag, Air/Light*, along with other literary magazines.
E: vexedlexpoetry@gmail.com
FB: @VexedLex
Instagrsm: @vexedlexpoetry

CULTURE

You don't speak Spanish?
Why didn't your mom teach you?
As if being Hispanic in America wasn't
Hard enough
Without my fellow Hispanics berating me
For not being in touch with my roots
The same roots that were embedded in American soul
They think I preferred to have learned the language
Of the world's conquerors
While their tongues are stained with Spanish blood
Spilled from centuries of slaughters.
As the daughter of a woman
Who juggled between the two tongues
You could say, I chose the lesser of two evils?
You have become reduced to the accent
Or lack thereof
That slips from a rehearsed tongue.
Puerto Ricans are losing their culture
According to who?
Because we love to listen to salsa and bachata too
We can suzy q on cue
But that is not enough
Until someone - a friend, a neighbour, a cousin
Can validate your Hispanic badge.

I LIKE TO PRETEND I'M PUERTO RICAN

Tomorrow is the Puerto Rican festival
And the day after that is the parade
So for these next two days
I can remember how I like to pretend I'm Puerto Rican
I can stroll through Spanish Harlem wearing my Puerto Rican shirt proudly
My chains and bracelets
Even my cap, depending on the temperature
I will bob my head to the beat of Rakata or Gasolina
Even Eso Eh
Because as a Puerto Rican in New York
As a Nuyorican
I was raised on Barrio Fino
Pa'l Mundo, Los Reyes del Perreo, Master Piece
I've got Marc Anthony and Frankie Negron programmed in my head
So that whenever I hear Vivir mi vida or te conozco bien
So that whenever I hear
Cara de nino or mi libertad
I can recite the lyrics
And pretend I'm Puerto Rican
I sing as much as I can remember
I don't have time to stop and actually understand what the words mean
At the festival, I can see the foods I refuse to eat
I've conditioned myself to sometimes eating arroz con pollo
And rarely, carne guisada
Each time I went into the cuchifritos with mom
I'd cringe at the display of the food
She'd salivate and tell me I'm missing out
She'd get on my case all the time about being a fake Puerto Rican
I'd argue that I'm only half
But yet, I haven't embraced my Venezuelan side either
I always thought that arguing with Dominicans and defending my honor was enough
I thought listening to Reggaeton from time to time was enough
I thought knowing Spanglish was enough
But I am a gringa
Who likes to pretend I'm Puerto Rican.

Joan McNerney
RAVENA, NEW YORK

Joan's poetry is found in many literary magazines such as *Seven Circle Press, Dinner with the Muse, Poet Warriors, Blueline*, and *Halcyon Days*. Four Bright Hills Press anthologies, several *Poppy Road* Journals, and numerous *Poets' Espresso Reviews* have also accepted her work. She has four Best of the Net nominations. Her latest titles are *The Muse in Miniature* and *At Work*.

E: poetryjoan@statetel.com

MY MOTHER

How she must have missed
those green hills of Ireland.
Walking along hard grey
streets in Brooklyn.

Remembering scent of
grassy meadows hurrying
along ten long blocks, to
climb filthy subway steps.

Missing those sweet soft pastures,
on her way home from work
buying day old bread, searching for
dented cans and items on sale.

Her marriage failed and her health
gone. Her smiling days were over.
No one seemed to care.
The unlucky are often alone.

How she must have longed
for songs around the fireplace.
Another Irish colleen torn
from that emerald island.

Anne Mitchell
CALIFORNIA

For Anne, the year 2020 gifted her solitude, a chance to slow down, observe and focus on her poetry. A year of Wild Writing Circles have been both anchor and flame for thoughts to flourish and become poems. Anne's recent work may be found in the *Community Journal* for writers.

E: annemitchell9@icloud.com

SONNET OF LOST SUMMERS

When days equal night and the air is crisp,
sand etches tides into swirls and I breathe
ferment of apples and hungry wasps' wisp,
before rushes of school bells greet pencils on leave.

Return of book bag and bike flaked in rust,
pack games in a trunk, with magic red knave,
cover in sheets 'til next season we trust,
during deep winter the screen porch you crave.

While lessons of Beowulf, Bio evolve,
surf sounds and waves seem forever on mute,
crosswords and crab feeds and beefsteaks dissolve
like elms out the window, barren in root.

Dark days of divorce in winter foment,
Summer cottage fades to forever's dormant.

A POEM ON IDENTITY HAS ME PERCHED ATOP AN EXISTENTIAL HIGH DIVE ...

To write about what formed me into this Anne
at a point in life sandwiched between passing of parents,
flyaway of a child, covid-era divorce by a notary
at the UPS store - I am faux introspection,

wandering in the rain, a stranger
in a seaside town, cupped hands to peek
in windows for signs of a warm
fire, a lure, but it's a bank holiday-all is dark.

Then, courage to put an eyeball through the mail slot-
first home on 3 Englewood Road, a probe for clues
of me hiding behind the gold fleur-de-lys wallpaper,
up the pulldown stairs Into the attic

where red felt doorknob covers
rest their ribbons and bells between Christmases
beside the coffin of my mother's childhood doll, Wendy Ann.
"Don't ever open that lid" we are told,

imaging porcelain bones concaved under her lace dress.
Summer heat fuels wasps to build their papery nests
in the eaves, dangling legs, little sabres
thwart attempts to peel open the yellowed tape

of old photo boxes, wedding albums. We don't sink
our faces into mothballed fur muffs,
or sparkle in the sequinned gowns
zipped up in quilted garment bags.

Once, I asked about Anne Lovelace,
two thirds of my name atop the calligraphied tree,
the one framed in silver over the radiator
by the front door, still dented from Dad's tumbler,

hurled on his way out. "She's the reason we are all here",
some widow heroine who writhed
in 17th century seas in a hold of puke and pee
to rock 8 children towards the land of Mary,

their heads still attached for a beach landing

in the estuary of the Chesapeake. "No relation",
I was told, later, when Nixon flooded through the Watergate
by way of a Deep Throat, a porn queen named Linda-

Yet the chortles come, the eyebrows raise,
I'm undressed with imagination at border crossings
on those first trips abroad-Lovelace it seems,
needs no translation.

I place her name in my Himitsu-Baku, Japanese
puzzle box- secret stash of love, wanderings, lost coins
of white magic Horcruxes bedded in Hakone walnut, cedar-
the mosaic's key a soulprint, my long slide through time.

Gena Williams
NORTH CAROLINA

Gena grew up in Georgia and moved to the North Carolina after retiring from her career as an elementary school teacher. She and her mother shared a love of writing both poetry and prose, mostly for their own enjoyment, but publishing a little along the way, too.
E: glw20x8rod@gmail.com
W: www.genawill.com
FB: @nelson.gena
Instagram: @genawilliams52

FOOTHILLS BACK PORCH GOOD MORNING

Coffee: hot, sweet, perfect.
Morning air, chilly
but with the promise of a beautiful day.
Also perfect.

Sunshine gently awakens
the hills across the way,
beams sliding down the hillsides
like children at play.

Even without looking,
I know the trees are happy.
How could they not be happy,
with a thousand trills of birdsong in their hair?

The gardenia is showing off again,
smiling from every blossom,
though I cannot see them from here.
There's no fragrance quite like gardenia
mixed with morning dew.
(Gardenias never travel incognito).

And Shisa's here, pressing
her warm muzzle into my hand,
saying good morning and that
she still loves me.
I bend and kiss
the top of her orange head
while she licks my fingers.
We both enjoy a small brain squishy,
then she wanders off the porch to the grass,
heeding Mother Nature's call
and to sniff the footprints of
the nighttime's visitors.
I put my bright blue coffee mug down and stretch –
a long, delicious, but oh, so gentle stretch –
arms out, legs out.
I could stretch a mile,
but I'd hate to have to walk back.
I settle for half a mile.

Then I reach for my black-and-white

plaid journal and my pen.
Open it to where the green ribbon is.

And the day has officially begun.

It's going to be a good one.

They all are, here in the foothills.

Donna Zephrine
NEW YORK

Donna was born in Harlem, and graduated from Columbia University School of Social Work in May 2017. She currently works for the New York State Office of Mental Health at Pilgrim Psychiatric Center Outpatient SOCR (State Operated Community Residence). She is a combat veteran who completed two tours in Iraq, stationed at Hunter Army Airfield 3rd Infantry Division as a mechanic. Since returning home, Donna enjoys sharing her experiences and storytelling through writing, and her stories have been published in the *New York Times, Writers Guild Imitative, Suicide, The Seasons, Lockdown, New World, Qutub Minar Review, Summer, War and Battle, Bards Initiative, Radvocate, Oberon, Long Island Poetry Association* and *The Mighty*. She has participated in various veteran writing workshops across NYC, was featured USA Warrior stories, and is involved in World Team Sports, Veteran of Foreign Wars, Wounded Warrior Project, Team Red, White & Blue, Team Rubicion, Project9line and Provetus, and serves on an advisory board for Heroes to Heroes.
E: kauldonna@yahoo.com

MY MIXED ANCESTRY CULTURAL HERITAGE

Coming from a unique nationality
African and East Indian heritage
I am very proud you see
Learning about my culture is something I like to do
My grandfather being Hindi
My grandmother had a Christian view
108 Mala beads means to me
Are inspirational prayers
My ex-husband from Kashmir taught me more about Hindi
While going to the Hindu Temple
Of Many, many gods
Mala beads become devotional mediation sample
Today I practice the Christian faith
In God I put my trust
Patiently in the Lord I decide to wait

Hanh Chau
CALIFORNIA

Born in Vietnam, of Chinese descent, Hanh has a Bachelor's and Master's degree in Business administration. During her spare time, she enjoys writing, listening to music and spending with her family.
E: hanhchau387@yahoo.com

I AM A WOMAN

I am a woman
shall not be afraid to be defined
By the color of my own skin
But solely by the content of character
And truth soul
I am who I am, by my integrity
To look far beyond
The superficial beauty
Through the inner view
I am a woman
With the privilege
That comes with carrying offspring
Inside a mother's womb
I am a woman
That is not petrified
To speak of her own mind
To stand up for what is right
I am a woman
That has lived through life
Walked in many other shoes
To understand the meaning
Of life
I am a woman
I may seem to be fragile
I've endured
Many battles of stormy weather
Day and night
rain and shine
But I never give up
to search for purpose
I am a woman
Portrayed as a delicate flower
I have never relinquished my beautiful title
I still stand tall
to carry my petals with
grace and pride
I am a woman standing strong
Conquering fear of all
Like a strenuous mountain
Conveying my message across world

Mark O. Decker
DELAWARE

Mark is a retired businessman, who started writing poetry beginning in 1968, and continues to the present. After retiring, in 2016, he decided to organize his life's work of poetry in order to preserve it for his children and grandchildren. As a result, he started self-publishing his poetry in 2016, and to-date has self-published fifteen books of poetry. He concurrently started sharing some of his poetry with his family and friends. Because of the very positive reaction he received about his poetry from family and friends, and through a writer's group he belongs to in Virginia and Delaware, he decided that he would share his words with a broader audience.

E: mdeckersr@gmail.com
FB: @Mark O. Decker Sr
Instagam: @Okeypoet

THE "I" IN ME

Except
for the song in my heart,
I hear no music;
Am I not alone?
Are we, each of us,
not abandoned, in some way,
pushed out, or running away,
to feel and find our own passage
to a place of peace and harmony;
Don't we all need
to follow Siddhartha's path
to enlightenment,
in a massive world,
that is exceedingly complex,
heartless, and
composed of inexplicables;
Life, really, is short, sweet and simple;
One might perceive
the contrary to be true;
It is not.

END

CULTURE & IDENTITY, Vol. 1 – WORLD

FEATURING:

J.P. Sexton - REPUBLIC OF IRELAND, Christopher Okemwa – KENYA, Tony Frisby – ENGLAND, Zohreh Baghban – IRAN, Gabriela Docan - ENGLAND / ROMANIA, Margarita Vanyova Dimitrova – BULGARIA, Syed Ahrar Ali – PAKISTAN, Eduard Harents – ALBANIA, Krishna Kumar Srinivasan – INDIA, Ndue Ukaj – KOSOVO, Rana Zaman – BANGLADESH, Mandy Macdonald – SCOTLAND, Xe M. Sánchez – SPAIN, Monique Holton – AUSTRALIA, Jen Ross – ARUBA, Jonathan Ukah – ENGLAND, Ali Alhazmi - SAUDI ARABIA, Monsif Beroual – MOROCCO, Brian Langley – AUSTRALIA, Bharti Bansal – INDIA, Amelia Fielden – AUSTRALIA, David Brady - PORTUGAL / ENGLAND, Jude Brigley – WALES, Fahredin Shehu – KOSOVO, Parthita Dutta - POLAND / INDIA, Amina Hrnčić - BOSNIA AND HERZEGOVINA, Hein Min Tun – MYANMAR, Hannah Gates - CHINA / ENGLAND, Eliza Segiet – POLAND, Xavier Panadès I Blas - CATALONIA (SPAIN), Bruce Louis Dodson – SWEDEN, Dariusz Pacak - AUSTRIA / POLAND, Rumyana Nikolova – BULGARIA, Francis Otole – NIGERIA, Lynn White – WALES, Stephen Kingsnorth – WALES, Sanjana Karthik - CANADA / INDIA, Cheryl-lya Broadfoot – ENGLAND, Jake Aller - SOUTH KOREA, Stefan Markovski - NORTH MACEDONIA, Ndaba Sibanda - ETHIOPIA / ZIMBABWE, Ioannis Adnan Karajoli - GREECE / SYRIA, Mark Andrew Heathcote – ENGLAND, Tetiana Grytsan-Czonka – UKRAINE, Kakoli Ghosh – INDIA, Neil Leadbeater – SCOTLAND, Masudul Hoq – BANGLADESH, Eduard Schmidt-Zorner - REPUBLIC OF IRELAND / GERMANY,NIvana Radojičić – SERBIA, John Tunaley – ENGLAND, Tanja Ajtic - CANADA / SERBIA, Aminath Neena – MALDIVES, Claudia Hardt - BAHRAIN / GERMANY, Chester Civelli – SWITZERLAND, Prof. Ron Roman - SOUTH KOREA, Rozalia Aleksandrova – BULGARIA, Zorica Bajin Đukanović – SERBIA, Volkan Hacıoğlu – TURKEY, Hussein Habasch - KURDISTAN / GERMANY, Tessa Thomson – ENGLAND, David A Banks – ENGLAND, Bhuwan Thapaliya – NEPAL, William Khalipwina Mpina – MALAWI, P. J. Reed – ENGLAND, George David – ROMANIA, Irma Kurti - ITALY / ALBANIA, Bill Cox – SCOTLAND, Dr. Ana Stjelja – SERBIA, Nivedita Karthik – INDIA, Ayesha Khurram – PAKISTAN, Rema Tabangcura - PHILIPPINES / SINGAPORE, Raji Unnikrishnan - BAHRAIN / INDIA, Kate Young – ENGLAND, Amrita Valan – INDIA, Alicia Minjarez Ramírez – MEXICO, Maja Herman-Sekuli – SERBIA, Maria Editha Garma-Respicio - HONG KONG / PHILIPPINES, Brajesh Singh – INDIA, James Aitchison – AUSTRALIA, Dr. Rehmat Changaizi – PAKISTAN, Alun Robert – ENGLAND, Ion-Marius Tatomir – ROMANIA, Mary Anne Zammit – MALTA, Monica Manolachi – ROMANIA, Igor Pop Trajkov - REPUBLIC OF NORTH MACEDONIA, Tanya A. Nikolova – BULGARIA, Miroslava

Panayotova – BULGARIA, Ewith Bahar – INDONESIA, Kathleen Boyle - VIETNAM / ENGLAND, Aleksandra Vujisić – MONTENEGRO, Máire Malone - ENGLAND / REPUBLIC OF IRELAND, Prafull Shiledar – INDIA, Tatyana Savova Yotova – BULGARIA, Dr. Sarah Clarke – ENGLAND, Shaswata Gangopadhyay – INDIA, Julie Ann Tabigne - SINGAPORE / PHILIPPINES and Dr. Archana Bahadur Zutshi – INDIA.

Printed in Great Britain
by Amazon